God Crushed Cancer
A Journal of My Faith Journey

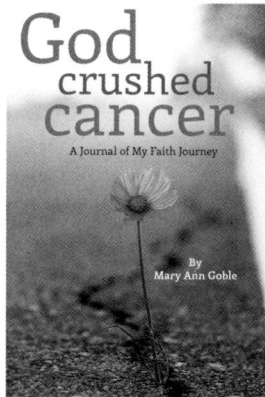

God
crushed
cancer
A Journal of My Faith Journey

By
Mary Ann Goble

By
MaryAnn Goble

For more information contact:
MaryAnn Goble
MaryAnnGoble@icloud.com
ISBN— 9798679980501
Printed in China
Formerly entitled Faith for the Journey
Back cover book description: Melissa Johnson
Photography © Danece Adams for DaneceAdamsPhotography.com

325
BOOKS
325BOOKS.COM

Dedication

To Kim Holmes, Christina Milan, and Kathy Connolly. Sisters and fellow warriors. Your faith lifted mine.

You have fought the good fight, You have finished the race, You have kept the faith. 2 Timothy 4:7 NKJV paraphrase

Contents

Acknowledgements

All my thanks and praise to my Lord, Jesus Christ. My strong tower, my refuge, my strength, and my cancer crusher! All glory to You, dear Savior, Healer, and King!

Love to my biggest fan and cheerleader, my husband Ed.

To my amazing and wonderful daughters, Kelly, Danece, and Melissa, thank you for your strong faith whenever mine may have been weak, and for always believing and never wavering. I love you.

To my dear Son's in Law, Matthew, David and Derick, I love you, thank you for supporting your wives, giving them the honor and value they deserve. You are very lucky men, if I say so myself!

To all my grand children who God has given me the honor to know, and love, and pour myself into. I love you, dear ones. You are my joys on earth, each one of you a unique and beautiful child of God. I thank God every day that I see you grow, and make good choices, and learn to know and love the Lord Jesus and His ways.

To my friends far and wide who have stood with me, cried with me, rejoiced with me, and believed with me, thank you. I love you and appreciate you so much. Let's pour some coffee or a glass of wine and do some porch sittin' real soon!

Blessings!

MaryAnn Goble

Forward

News of malignant cancer will rock a stable soul, halt momentum, and slam on the brakes of a fast-moving life. That's what happened to us. To MaryAnn, specifically, my dear wife.

MaryAnn has always been a fighter. She is the type of person who loves others deeply, especially her family, and will jump into any scuffle, to help them, to stand up for what is right, to defend and protect. She should wear a badge. One with a mama bear on it.

We hadn't noticed the knot forming in her breast. By the time we did, the evil mass was found to be quickly growing, infecting every cell it could reach, as if in a race to see how much it could consume get before being caught.

By God's grace, MaryAnn was led to the right doctors, each one, with great empathy, dealing directly, quickly, and resolutely, with the issue at hand—exactly as MaryAnn would want them to—black and white, no shades of gray. She asked, "What is it? How do we get rid of it? And how do we keep it from ever coming back?"

Her surgeon, the renown Dr. Anees Chagpar, drew up options for us, and, prayerfully, MaryAnn decided on the most aggressive approach. The first time we met with Dr. Chagpar, we knew she was the person God was going to use, when she said, "You know those Breast Cancer Runs with the ladies wearing the 15-year, and 25-year Survivor tee-shirts?" We nodded. "That's what I do," she said. "You came to the right place." You could almost hear the Rocky Theme playing as she hugged my tearful, smiling, wife.

Over the next year there were surgeries and chemotherapy treatments, radiation, and sickening medication. In addition to Dr. Chagpar, MaryAnn was equally blessed to come under the oncology care of Dr. Dharamvir Jain, who would shepherd her medications going forward. And, just this fall, around nine years after it all started, Dr. Jain confirmed MaryAnn's all-clear status—which he had monitored since 2011.

We are grateful for the services of these and other caregivers, especially, nurse Juliet, who became a confidant, and trusted friend, through the process.

Interestingly, though, as miserable as MaryAnn was through much of the first year, faith kindled into a flame in her heart, as she discovered a depth of life with her Lord, Jesus Christ, that she didn't know existed. What her enemy had meant for evil, to destroy her and crush her faith, backfired, as she fell into the loving arms of Jesus, Who held her and gave her the confidence and strength to fight back. She would say, "I know I'm going to die, we all are. But I'm *not* going to die from *this*. No way. God is my healer." And no circumstance or diagnosis could move her from that foundation of faith. She knew, that she knew, that she knew.

Her faith is big, pure. Real. I'm proud of her, I'm amazed by her, and I'm so glad she wrote her blog through the first season of treatment. It is raw, and honest, and I hope the people who read it, whether or not they are facing a demon like cancer, will discover for themselves the deep relationship with God that MaryAnn found. Then, as she does daily, live life with the invincible confidence that, *"If God is for you, who can be against you?"*

Ed Goble

MaryAnn Goble

God Crushed Cancer
A Journal of My Faith Journey

God Can Do Anything, But Fail

1/20/2010

Ed and I have great memories of singing this song to our kids, and of his mom singing the song to his younger sisters. All children should learn this song so later, if they ever face a diagnosis like I did, the Lord can bring it back to their minds, as He graciously did for me, and they will remember Who is in charge.

God can do anything, anything, anything
God can do anything but fail
God can do anything, anything, anything
God can do anything but fail

But Jesus looked at them and said to them, "With men this is impossible, but with God all things are possible." Matthew 19:26 NKJV

Blessings

Hope For The Season

1/26/2010

Danece and I were talking yesterday about how God made the seasons and how they will always change, they come when they are supposed to, and accomplish their intended purpose. God is amazing like that. Of course, some of the seasons aren't very pleasant, especially when it's extra hot or so cold your eyelashes freeze. Seasons of life can be that way, too. Hot, cold, pleasant or downright painful, affecting both you and the people around you. It's not that God causes the trouble that seasons sometimes bring, but more that He is sovereign over each facet of His creation and uses every season to miraculously bring glory to Christ. And, seasons are temporary! They are always changing! They last for a while and then they change. Another season, one more pleasant, or, one even tougher, is sure to follow—all spinning to the eventual and certain return of the King of Kings.

The seasons of our lives are part of that Romans 8:28 promise we stand firmly upon.

And we know that all things work together for good to those who love God, to those who are the called according to His purpose. Romans 8:28 NKJV

There is a passage in Revelation where Jesus is writing to a persecuted church. This group of people were in a really rough season as the enemy pressed them on every side. Jesus said that this season would last "for ten days" (Revelation 2:10). Ed and I have always wondered what that meant, exactly. It could be a literal ten-day period, obviously, or it could mean something more symbolic. But the exciting thing is that it is Jesus who established the duration, not Satan. The season they were in was rough, and it would last ten days, but it wouldn't last eleven. It would not last one minute longer than Jesus dictated, because He is Lord of Lords.

If I were in that church and read that message from Jesus, at first, I might have been a little depressed, realizing that my deliverance would not be immediate. But then, maybe after the truth of God's love sunk into my heart and spirit, I would say, "Wait a minute, I can make it ten days! If Jesus has dictated ten days for this season, then bring it on!"

For me, this season may be just beginning, I might be on "Day One", so to speak. But I know that Jesus defines the limit of this season, not Satan. I can rest in that. I have a Father in heaven who loves me, and He is not surprised by the season at all. He knows. My husband (my best friend), and I are going through this season together, and with God and Ed on my side, I know I will make it! We can do anything for ten days!

Blessings

He Is My Healer

1/27/2010

I have been rejoicing since about 4:30 p.m. yesterday afternoon! My appointment was at 2:00, but as it is sometimes with Doctor's, we waited a while... My mind had plenty of time to wander in that Time. Danece was with us as we went to the doctor's office. On the way there, I said I was reminded that Jesus is holding onto to me. I am in His hands! She asked me afterward what I was thinking before I saw the doctor. I told her that at first, I was extremely confident. Then, as time went by, I had moments of "What if?" My husband was there to hold me, and though I had those "what if" thoughts, I know Whom I have believed! I was reminded that Jesus was holding me as well, and nothing can snatch us from His hand!

I give them eternal life, and they will never perish. No

one can snatch them away from me, for my Father has given them to me, and He is more powerful than anyone else. No one can snatch them from the Father's hand. John 10:28-29 NLT

It was important for Jesus that we know this! He said it twice, one right after the other! He loves us! He loves me! No one can snatch me from the Father's hand! I can rejoice in that, and rest in that! I need this promise right now! I am so thankful that He helps us to recall His promises, because He loves us.

The news was great! As we, and many others had been praying, and believing it would be. The cancer is contained. It hasn't spread! Amen and Amen! I believe that Jesus can heal all my disease! It is up to Him how that happens. I am holding on to Him, and I know He is holding me. The news was music to my ears. I still have to go through a course of treatment, but as I wrote yesterday, it is just for a season. He is my Healer!

So the next part of the journey begins.

Blessings

I Feel Small

1/29/2010

Today I feel really small. I felt something under my eye earlier, I wiped at it with a finger and found a tiny little speck of something. That little grain of makeup or sand or whatever it was kind of describes how I am feeling. A small, insignificant little speck.

A grain of irritating sand on the face of the universe. There are billions of specks like me on the earth. So why do I matter? What's the big deal about my life? Have you ever felt like this? Overwhelmed by your place in this vast desert of sand, each grain basically like those all around it? My husband is claustrophobic and today I kind of relate to how he feels. Alone, yet surrounded. Small. Overmatched.

Then I think about God and sigh. The few things I

know about Him remind me that He doesn't see me the way I see myself. He sees me as if I were the only person in the world. He sees me as if I'm the only person that matters to Him. He loves me so much that He would have died for my sin had I been the only person that was lost. He knows every thought, every detail, every hurt and tear. And He loves me more than I will ever comprehend. He chose me and He has a destiny and a purpose for my life - I have a reason, lots of them, for living strong and confident in Him!

Today this is all a little hard for me to comprehend. What could be so unique and loveable about this little speck when there are over thousands, just like me that have lost their lives in an earthquake, with hundreds of thousands more that are injured, homeless and hungry - not knowing what tomorrow will bring, let alone next month or next year.

Surely God is putting all His attention to the hearts cry of the Haitian people. Right? Well, if I understand it correctly, that is true, but not in the way we would normally think.

Yes, He is focusing all His attention on Haiti right now, but He is also focusing all His attention on me, and He is focusing all His attention on you and the issues you are dealing with, and He is focusing all His attention on the people in China and Ethiopia and every single little speck on the earth, from the babies just conceived and growing in a mother's womb, to the oldest nomad roaming around herding flocks in the desert. How? I have no idea. But I know it's true because He is God and that's what He does.

So today I'll put my feelings aside and operate instead from what I know to be true. That God loves me, this little speck in central Kentucky with breast cancer. This little speck that has a family that loves her and friends that pray for her and doctors that care for her. And, especially, a God that is focused on her and loves her very, very much. Amen!

Blessings

You Paid It All

1/31/2010

Today as I stand and look at the road ahead, it seems very long. How ever I am feeling, I am choosing to remember that Jesus paid the price for me, once and for all! I will choose to stand with Him and trust Him! Please enjoy this reminder of the once-for-all gift given to each of us from our Lord, Jesus Christ.

I hear the savior say
Thy strength indeed is small
Child of weakness watch and pray
Find in me thine all in all
Jesus paid it all, all to Him I owe.
Sin had left a crimson stain,
He washed it white as snow.

Blessings

The Waiting Game
2/3/2010

Of all the games that we play in life, the Waiting Game is the worst. At least for me it is and I would guess that I'm not alone. I waited around for a diagnosis and now that we have it, I'm ready to fight. I want to get going, get on with stuff, tests, treatments, whatever it takes, I'm ready to get this icky garbage out of my body!

But instead, I wait... Can you relate with me on this?

I told Ed that I wished it was October already because they told us this would be an 8-or-9-month process, so man I'm already counting the days and I want it done, you know?

I guess waiting is important sometimes, though. Isaiah encouraged it when he said,

But those who wait on the Lord
Shall renew their strength;
They shall mount up with wings like eagles,
They shall run and not be weary,
They shall walk and not faint. Isaiah 40:31 NKJV

So I know it's the right thing to do and that everything has a time and a season, Solomon taught us that.

We're seeing great doctors, we're in good hands, we're trusting the Lord and enjoying the encouragement and support of family and friends, and I know we'll get through this. Being impatient about it won't get me anything but stirred up, and I'm a redhead, so you know I can get stirred up!

So here's how I want to be right now - instead of twiddling my thumbs waiting for the phone to ring to schedule my next whatever, I want to:

- Rest in the Lord, and watch as He orchestrates every detail

- Enjoy this intimate time with the Lord, feeling His loving touch and encouraging voice of scripture

- Encourage people to seek Him and trust Him

- Be reminded of His promises and stand on them

- Display patience, a virtue that works like a "Get Out Of Jail Free" card in the Waiting Game

- See each day as an opportunity to be a blessing to someone

- Bask in the love of my husband and girls

- Give God glory for each season, even the Waiting Game season!

Blessings

How Quickly We Forget

2/5/2010

The children of Israel were stuck in Egypt enslaved to a pharaoh who saw them as a free labor force. They cried out to God from their bondage and He heard them—He always does.

He sent Moses to deliver them and in the familiar story about the plagues God sent upon Egypt because Pharaoh wouldn't let the people go, we read how all the creepy-crawlies and gooey, weird stuff happened to the people of Egypt, but not the Israelites. God even kept the gnats from bugging them. Eventually, after the ultimate plague when the angel of death visited the homes of Egypt, Pharaoh let the people go, actually, he pretty much begged them to leave. A while later Pharaoh had a change of heart, he wanted his labor force back, so he decided to chase them down with an army of chariots.

How quickly we forget.

Didn't he remember who he was dealing with here? Didn't he remember how it felt to have his land visited by the One True God?

God delivered Israel from Pharaoh's hand, again, and they crossed the sea and headed for the promised land. It didn't take long for them to grow weary, though, and start complaining about their situation there, wandering around in the desert. They decided that it was better back in Egypt.

How quickly we forget.

Didn't they remember the pain and suffering under Pharaoh's hand? Didn't they remember crying out to God to deliver them - and how He answered their cry? Didn't they remember the plagues and look over and see their firstborn sons and recall how God spared them and redeemed them all? He didn't send them back to Egypt, He knew what was best, and while their sin kept most of them from entering the promised land, future generations would enjoy the fruit of their deliverance in that fateful season.

How quickly we forget, but God never does.

I look back over the past couple of months and see God's protection and love for me and my family. When I look at past trials, I can see how God lovingly brought me through. Then, I get the diagnosis that I have can-cer and my world starts to spiral again. But wait, I look back and can see His hand working, clearly protect-ing me, watching me, caring for me, loving me. And I know He hasn't changed, Hebrews says:

Jesus Christ is the same yesterday, today, and forever. Hebrews 13:8 NKJV

If He delivered me then, if He heard my hearts cry then, will He not hear me now, in this new season, in this unfamiliar valley? Of course, He will!

How quickly we forget!

I am going to stand on the promise that He will never leave me or forsake me and remember all the times He has shown Himself strong on my behalf and on be-half of my family. I'm going to ask Him to bring those things to my mind each time I start to look around and complain about my health or whatever is bugging me next time. God is with me, His word is true, He deliv-ered me then, and He'll do it again!

I'll try not to forget so quickly next time!

Blessings

Ready, set, Go!

2/8/2010

Things are starting to happen pretty quickly now. I have a biopsy and a port put in tomorrow, this is some little gizmo they surgically implant to administer the chemo drugs, so they don't have to go hunting and pecking for a good vein every time. Then, on Friday, I have a heart test to make sure my heart is strong enough for chemo, followed next week, probably Wednesday, with 8 rounds of chemo, (one treatment every two weeks).

After that they give my body a few weeks to rest and then we do it all over again with a different set of drugs. After that, I guess time will tell.

I am so blessed to have the love of my husband, and girls, and so many friends! I also am very blessed to know that God is mindful of me. He loves me, and hears the cries of my heart! There is nothing that can separate me from His love—I am ready to win this! So, ready, set, Go!

Yet in all these things we are more than conquerors through Him who loved us. For I am persuaded that neither death nor life, nor angels nor principalities nor powers, nor things present nor things to come, nor height nor depth, nor any other created thing, shall be able to separate us from the love of God which is in Christ Jesus our Lord. Romans 8:38-39 NKJV

Blessings

Life And Healing

2/15/2010

My child, pay attention to what I say. Listen carefully to my words. Don't lose sight of them. Let them penetrate deep into your heart, for they bring life to those who find them, and healing to their whole body. Proverbs 4:20-22 NLT

Some people believe the Bible is outdated, historical literature. I've never understood this viewpoint as the Bible claims to be God's Word to mankind—all of us. With all its internal and external evidence, including the resurrection of Jesus Christ from the dead, what more should we need—that's good enough for me and more than I deserve.

But as important as it is to realize that the Good Book is God's Word, it is even more important for the Word to be read and to become part of our lives. He wants

His word to penetrate deep into our hearts—I love that! To me that suggests that we should hide it deeply into our hearts, letting it touch every part with God's breath and voice. If we do His promise is life and healing, actually, healing to our whole body! Now that's good medicine!

I read that if we are given a prescription for a particular condition, but never take it, then we can't expect it to do what the doctor said it would. It is the same with His Word. If we just believe in it, but never let it penetrate us, then how can we expect to receive its promises?

I want God's Word to have its full reign in my life and body and for it to accomplish everything God desires it to because of my faith in His grace and power.

My prayer is that we will recognize how important it is to hide His Word in our hearts! He sees my struggle right now, and the need I have for physical healing.

I trust Him! I need His strength right now. I am going to go read more "life" and "healing" words right now from the scriptures - and, let them penetrate deeply into my heart. Join me?

Your word I have hidden in my heart, That I might not sin against You. Psalm 119:11 NKJV

Blessings

One Down, Seven To Go

2/18/2010

Yesterday was my first round of chemo. It was a full day, because we attended a chemotherapy class, and then had a consultation with the Radiation doctor. Each and every person we have encountered at the Brown Cancer Center has been amazing. I was one of the last patients to receive chemo for the day, so it could have felt hurried or like I was keeping the staff from going home after a long day, but I never felt that. My time was very relaxed, and I could just tell that everyone coming through the doors to the chemo chairs is treated like they are the most important person in the world. It was wonderful.

My treatment went well and so far not much nausea, which is one thing we've heard a lot. I am sure as the drugs build up in my system it could be different, but so far so good. My prayer as I go to every doctor's visit, or chemo treatment, is that I can shine the light of Jesus to everyone I meet.

Yesterday it seemed most people had someone with them, while at another doctor visit I noticed quite a few people coming alone. I hope I am able to love people with the love of the Lord and show them that not only do the doctors and nurses care, but so do I! More importantly, God loves them so much, and cares about them more than anyone ever will!

So, one down, and seven to go. Eight chemo treatments in total. I can do this! I can beat this!

Thank you for praying with and for us, and when you think of it, pray also for a cure to the various kinds of cancer that people are dealing with every day.

Blessings

My Best Days are Ahead of Me

2/19/2010

Okay, it's my birthday. I'm, uh, one year older than my last birthday... Anyway, Ed bought the single from Danny Gokey for me for my birthday, and it's right where I'm at today, *"My Best Days are Ahead of Me"*. I am standing firm in this! I know through God nothing is impossible, and I truly believe the best days of my life are ahead of me! I admit, I would probably rather fast forward nine months to when this process will be over, but I am on this journey, and every day is important and every day I get to discover something about myself and about the Lord. And, every day I might have an opportunity to be a blessing to someone, and I wouldn't want to miss that. I don't mind at all being another year older!

Blessings

My Shelter
2/22/2010

The Lord is my rock and my fortress and my deliverer; The God of my strength, in whom I will trust: My shield and the horn of my salvation, My stronghold and my refuge; My Savior, You save me from violence. 2 Samuel 22:2-3 NKJV

Yesterday as we went to church, I was a little nervous. Not about going to church, I love that, love the people and the worship and the whole thing. It's just that the doctors told me that my immune system will be weak through this process of chemotherapy. I was a little nervous because of the thought that I might love on someone who didn't know they were contagious with something, and I would be more easily exposed than usual.

Isn't it funny how our mind works? I've never worried

about that kind of thing before. I felt kind of silly, really. But the feeling was real, silly or not. Well, after the (long) greeting time and I hugged about half the people in Marion County, we sang one of my favorite songs, *Make Me Glad*. The chorus was a word from the Lord straight to my heart, it says:

> *You are my shield, My strength, My portion,*
> *Deliverer My shelter, Strong tower*
> *My very present help in time of need*

I needed to be reminded that HE is my shelter. The dictionary describes the word shelter as "a covering, or refuge." Yes, my immune system may be weak, but God is my Shelter! He is my covering and my refuge. He knows exactly what my body can or cannot take. Should I be cautious? of course, but not to the point of not relying on the shelter of the Lord!

I think of how a mother duck takes care of her young. If she thinks they are in danger or need of protection, she covers them! I love the idea that my Father in Heaven does the same thing with mercy and tenderness. Even when I might be exposed to something that I am not aware of, I am safe with Him, safe under His wing.

One of the many friends who are praying for me, said; "May the Lord who brought you this far, watch over every cell in your body!" What a great thought!

Because this battle is taking place within my cells, on a tiny, internal battlefield. Amen. I am trusting this! God is watching over every single cell in my body, like He watches over every sparrow in the sky, which are HUGE compared to a human cell! His grace is covering me like a strong tower against any storm.

Blessings

My Love
2/23/2010

Today I just want to write a Thank You!

First to my God! You are my Healer. I know this. I am constantly assured of this! I have nothing to fear! I would rather be in Your loving, strong arms, than anywhere else! I know Your plans for me are better than anything I can imagine, even in this valley called cancer. Thank You, Lord!

I felt like I wanted to write a note to say Thank You to my husband, Ed. Oh the stories I could tell... Like a few months after we got married, I was going through a fast food restaurant, and ran the side of our car right down the poll that is supposed to protect the building from cars getting too close.

Well, it did protect the building, I guess.

How about the time during the midst of a little argument, I almost started the kitchen on fire? He saved the day and protected our home.

Or the time we received a brand-new car from someone for our ministry, and I totaled it in the first month!

He stood with me when I gave birth to our three girls and was even there when I miscarried a couple of times. He took care of me when I got the mumps from a mission trip that we took together. I know I wasn't a very good patient then, because it really hurt!

Or how about all the times he listened patiently while I cried about something that, in hindsight, was pretty silly. Or how much he cared when I wanted to tell him about some little nothing event from my day.

When I think of this man the Lord has blessed me with, I am amazed! He has such a heart for the Lord. He wants everyone to know the Lord. He spent a good portion of our life seeking to point people to the Lord, and still does! His desire is for people to see Jesus. He is always helping people see who Jesus is, and how much He loves them, no matter what they have done. He never expects someone to do something that he would not do himself. He would gladly give you his last dollar, or the shirt off of his back, if you needed it. And that's not just a cliche, he's done it. A lot.

When I think of our love, I am overwhelmed. He loves me no matter what. He has forgiven me big things, and little things. He has shown me over and over that he only wants me, and his love for me is deeper than I can ever understand. Sometimes in the morning, I want to write him a note to tell him how much I love him, and the words just don't seem big enough. Every time he writes me a love letter however, he amazes me with how special he makes me feel, by the number of different ways he can assure me he loves me!

I am a very blessed woman to have this man for my husband. He is the love of my life! I love sharing our quiet moments together, and also those times when the whole family is together, and it is very, very loud! I love the simple things he brings me, like his smile, his eyes, his laugh, his heart—these are gifts for me, and I will always treasure these gifts from the Lord!

I don't like having cancer. I don't like putting the love of my life through this. However, I can't imagine anyone that I would rather have holding me through this, than my husband Ed. I may have written this before, but its so true: With God, and Ed, walking with me through this, I am in great hands, and know I will win this!

Thank you, my love.

Blessings

Children

2/25/2010

Ever since I was a little girl I wanted to be a mommy. No big world-changing plans or dreams, except maybe to become President, which I would be really good at, by the way. Mostly, I just wanted to be somebody's mommy. I have always loved kids. There's just something about those smelly, dirty-faced little boys and prissy, pretty little girls that is just so innocent and wonderful. It's the twinkle in their eyes as they work through something that's just outside their grasp. It's the mischief on their face as they ponder grabbing a fresh cookie off the counter. It's their simple, amazing faith.

Kids love learning and exploring and discovering new things. Some of them will try anything and would leap into your arms from ten feet away if you said you would catch them. They trust and they love, and they haven't a care in the world. They look up to us big people and they strive to please and to be good, even when it's hard. They demonstrate love through simple things, they don't have money, so they can't try and buy affection, they can just hug and cuddle and smile and kiss and be polite. Their reward is approval, and sometimes a treat.

Teaching kids at Sunday School was such a joy. To watch as the stories of Jesus came to life and they realized how much God loved them.

That happened to me at about age ten when I began to understand that Jesus loved me—loved me so much that He died for my sins. I didn't really understand that part at the time, but I sure do now, boy do I! And I'm still amazed by it!

Over the past few days I've gotten calls and notes from parents and caregivers that have assured me that their kids are praying for me. Wow, what an honor! Because I know that kids really know how to pray. Their prayers are so confident and powerful because of their absolute, simple faith. They have no doubt that God will answer their prayers, why wouldn't He, He's God!

One child put it like this, "God is amazing, and He will heal you." Amen! Thank you, little friend, I receive that!

Oh, how I want to have that kind of faith! The kind we have before life begins to take it's twists and turns. Jesus said we could, actually, that we would have to in order to inherit His kingdom. Funny, but I find myself getting more childlike every day, not in my immaturity, although that might be debated, but more in my faith and trust that God has started a good work in me. It started when I was a little girl, continues today and He has promised to complete it in my life. In my case that will take a while, a good long while, so I know I'll be around for a long, long time! By God's grace and the prayers and support of my friends, little and big... Thank You!

...being confident of this very thing, that He who has begun a good work in you will complete it until the day of Jesus Christ. Philippians 1:6 NKJV

Blessings

Let's Hear It For The Girls!

2/26/2010

When God decided that man needed someone by his side to help him, He was right as rain. Women are amazing! Women can leap tall buildings in a single bound! Sometimes I believe we must be super-human, because of all the things that women do. Some are teachers, others are stay-at-home moms, administrators, hostesses, waitresses, nurses, doctors, professors, work for the police force, lawyers, congress, senate, sales—the list is endless. Actually, at some point in our lives we probably function in all of these "jobs" in some form! Women can do anything they set their mind to.

If we become a mom, what we do becomes even more amazing! God is good, because in designing us, He gives us what we need to function as a mom should. He prepared our bodies to be able to carry children until they are born into this world. He also designed our emotional and mental capacities to take care of our children. And He gives us help in His Word for when our life seems overwhelming. Women love deeply, try to see the best in people, protect like a bear, put others first. Women don't want someone to tell us we can't do something—that just makes us crazy, and we will figure out how to do whatever that is no matter what!

I am very fortunate to have some wonderful women in my life! Some of them working outside the home, and others not. Some though they work outside the home, when they get home, they do another full day's work before they go to bed at night. Some of them moms, others not yet. These women God has given to me as family and friends, are wonderful. My own daughters are approaching Sainthood, I think! My daughters show me every day what women can do! They don't know the word, can't for one minute. They are becoming more and more like Jesus every day! Truly beautiful women of God!

I also have very close "girlfriends", some family some not, that I wouldn't know what to do if they weren't in my life! They love me, and tell me when I am being stupid, and love me some more! I am a very blessed woman. I am so thankful for these women!

Mostly women are attacked by the type of cancer I

have. What I want to say to you is this... Take the time to do all you can do to stay healthy. Does that make it so you won't get this? No. I thought I was doing all the "right stuff". The fact we live in a fallen world, and sickness happens, is just the way things are. But if it does happen to you, (I am praying every day that it doesn't!), take it like a woman! Be the strong woman of God that He made you to be! Don't listen to people who tell you, you can't beat this! Not true! Especially if you are holding on to the Creator of women!

Hold on to His Hand, and run right through those walls the enemy puts up to stop you! You are amazing! God made you that way!

We ought and indeed are obligated [as those in debt] to give thanks always to God for you, brethren, as is fitting, because your faith is growing exceedingly and the love of every one of you each toward the others is increasing and abounds. 2 Thessalonians 1:3 AMP

I am very thankful for y'all! What a blessing it is for me to have such wonderful women of God surrounding me with love and prayer! My prayer is that every day we are stretched and molded by our Lord and Savior. May your faith this week grow beyond measure, and may you see the love God has for you in a very new and special way.

MaryAnn Goble

I love you girls very much, thank you for being such a wonderful part of God's work in my life.

Blessings

Feelings and Saturday Morning

2/27/2010

The past three days I have felt pretty good! Almost like normal! Feeling good can fool me. I try and do everything I want to get done, and don't pace myself, and then I am shaky and weary... not so good. But I like feeling good, even if it means I need to be a little more careful with my activity for a while. I have to listen to all of you who have been telling me to listen to my body. Okay, lesson learned.

I woke up this morning, Saturday, and watched my love sleeping, and then noticed it was snowing outside. I love this kind of morning! No rush to get to the doctor, or the workplace. The peacefulness of a slow morning is something I have learned to really enjoy. I love to be inside, all warm and cozy with a cup of coffee, my hubby with me, watching the snow fall! In the summer we spend mornings like this on the porch in the rockers, but not today, too cold for these bones!

Thank you, Lord for helping me to feel good! Thank you, Lord for healing me! In Jesus Name, AMEN!

Blessings

Number Two

3/1/2010

Just a couple more days until my second treatment.
I think I am ready physically and mentally. It seems
like they are checking my blood for this and that about
every five seconds and so far it's been really good
each time. I've been feeling really good, too, but how
could I not feel good with a cook like my husband
around—I'm thinking of his soon-to-be-world-famous,
smashed-blueberry pancakes last night—yum!

As Chemo 2-of-8 approaches, there are a couple of
things that I am praying for:

- That the love of Jesus overflows my heart in the
  treatment room to be a blessing to each person I
  encounter.

- That the drugs do what they are designed to do,

seek and destroy the cancer cells.

- That all the innocent, good cells in my body that are minding their own business and doing what they're supposed to will be protected and made strong by the Lord of my body - it is the temple of the Holy Spirit, after all!

May God receive great glory throughout this process. He is worthy! Thank you again to everyone who is praying for me!

Blessings

You're Getting Sleeeepyyyy...

3/5/2010

Wow! I didn't see this one coming... I asked the chemo nurse if I could expect the same level of side-effects for the rest of the cycle that I experienced after the first treatment and she said, "Yes, for the most part." And my side-effects were minimal, so I was pretty happy with her prediction.

But about five minutes after the treatment was over I started to feel just drained, pooped, wore-out, you know? Like I just needed a nap. Famous last words, as they say, because except for a few brief seasons of consciousness, I pretty-much slept for the next 24 hours! Unreal! I just couldn't wake up. Last night I kept waking briefly to tell Ed I was sorry for sleeping all the time, I felt so lazy. He assured me that it was okay, but still. He nudged me at 10:00 and said Rascal Flatts (one of my favorite groups) was on CSI (one of my favorite shows) and I fought my way out of the comma long enough to watch that, but then it was straight to bed! Amazing!

Chemotherapy can be so draining! I've heard that from other cancer patients and now I know firsthand that it is true. I guess it makes sense since there is a literal war going on in your body as the chemo is trying to seek out and destroy the cancer cells, while your body, in defense mode, is trying it's hardest to fight against this foreign invader. It's almost non-sensical, they put bad stuff in to destroy the bad stuff that's already in there.

But the bad stuff that's already in there (the cancer) is sneaky and posing as innocent little cells, like my hair cells, or skin cells or mucus cells. The chemo drugs can't tell the difference between all those fast-dividing cells, so it just goes after them all. Well, God designed super-soldiers in the blood to rise up and protect the hair, skin and mucus, all the cells that can't stand up for themselves—so the fight is on! And it absolutely wears you out!

The good news is that God is in charge, He is Lord of my body, this little frame is the Temple of the Holy Spirit. So I trust Him to protect the innocent, good cells, and point the chemo medicine accurately toward the breast cancer, find it and destroy it, wherever it is hiding in there. God can do that because He is God!

It feels good to have treatment #2 done! There are two more in this cycle, then they change the medicine, and then four more of that kind, "T" something... God is sustaining me through this and healing me! Thanks for all the prayers!

This is the verse that I found comforting this morning:
Wealth and honor come from you alone, for you rule over everything. Power and might are in your hand, and at your discretion people are made great and given strength. 1 Chronicles 29:12 NLT

He is giving me strength! Without it, I would not be able to stand. Thank you Lord!

Blessings

New Every Morning

3/9/2010

In my little world, there is a lot going on! A war going on in my body, that I am sure the Lord will have victory over! Sometimes it seems it will last so long. I know however, that this is just a season. A rough one, but still just a season. There are also many blessings in my life! We received great news from the doctor, the cancer is shrinking! Praise the Lord! My husband who wakes up every morning and tells me how beautiful I am, and how much he loves me more every day! I love him more than I can ever say.

My oldest daughter, Kelly, who amazes me at being such a great mom and professional. She accomplishes more in 5 minutes, than most people do in a day! She is a blessing to her husband, boys, parents, sisters, and friends!

My second daughter, Danece, is in charge of a bunch of wonderful interns at her church, and also Children's Church. When she found out that I had cancer, she prayed and felt like the Lord wanted her to come home here to Kentucky and take care of me while I went through treatment, whatever that involved. All my girls would do this if they could, that is how wonderful they are, and how lucky I am! Danece continued to pray about it, and finally approached her leaders at work. They agreed with her!

So, she will be coming home to be with me while I am getting better! I am excited to have her here and know the sacrifice she is making!

My youngest daughter, Melissa, is finishing school in California, and working hard to have a little cash on hand while she is there. We found out that I had cancer right after she left to go back to school. It made it so hard for her to stay and apply herself toward school when she felt like she wanted to be home with me during this time. However, we knew this was what the Lord had in mind for her to do. She is a great student, a hard worker, and a wonderful friend! I miss her but will get to see her in May!

My girls are beautiful and love the Lord with all their heart! I can't say enough how proud I am of them!

If we take just a minute to look around us, we can see

the wonderful blessings the Lord gives us every day. They are new every morning! I know that we all have trials to deal with, it is part of life. However, let's focus on the blessings! This will help us get through the trials with patience, and love, and maybe even some joy from the Lord! My prayer for y'all is wrapped up in this verse:

May The Lord bless you and protect you. May the Lord smile on you and be gracious to you. May the Lord show you His favor and give you His peace. Numbers 6:24-26 NLT

Blessings

People, People Who Need People
3/11/2010

Wasn't that a Barbara Streisand song? *"People, people who need people, are the luckiest people, in the world..."* We do need each other, and we need Jesus, too. You can tell that in about five seconds if you, like me, are a people-watcher.

I like to go to the mall and people-watch. Actually, just about any public place will do. The king of all days to go people-watching, of course, is the day after Thanksgiving. These people, and I am one of them, are proof that God has a great sense of humor.

When I think about some of the dumb things I have done, I smile when I think about how God might look at me, and sometimes I cry, because I know I have disappointed Him. The truth is that God loves people even when we don't have a clue! Not only that, His love is unconditional. It doesn't matter how many times we booger something up, God is never going to stop loving us.

My hope is that someday I can see people the way God does, and I can learn to love the way He does. When God designed people, He made each one unique. No one acts, thinks, or feels, quite the same way I do. That fact also makes for pretty interesting relationships.

Sometimes it is hard for us to love people. We can be so selfish sometimes we don't think about how we are affecting others. We go into a restaurant and our server doesn't approach with a smile so we decide to not tip them well, because they didn't please us. We don't stop to think this person might be going through some terrible trial in their life, and it is all they can do to get up every morning and get themselves out the door to work. Sometimes our focus is so narrowly selfish that it is impossible to see others and be the blessing God wants us to be.

Society today suggests that we should only look out for ourselves, it is even taught to our children. God gave us each other to have relationship. He knew from the beginning that we would need others. He wanted relationship with us, and He also wanted us to cultivate our relationships with others. He tells us time and again, putting others first is the best way to have relationships. We all want to be loved, and you can just tell when someone is truly interested in what you are going through. We know when it is not "all about them!" We need to be careful that isn't "all about us" either. Putting others first seems to be easy enough, and yet this struggle is huge in our society.

There is nothing more important in our lives than our relationship with God, and our relationships with others! My prayer is I can learn to see people and love them the way God does. I don't want to focus only on what I am going through, but help others who are dealing with the same thing, or another trial in their life.

People have drifted so far away from God, and they don't know how much He loves them, or desires a relationship with them! Would you help me point others to the love God has for them? Can we step outside of ourselves long enough to help someone in need? God wants everyone to know Him!

For God so loved the world that He gave His one and only Son, that whoever believes in Him shall not perish but have eternal life. John 3:16 NIV

Blessings

Feeling So Loved!
3/15/2010

I had a great week with Danece and Ed. Sunday morning brought another special blessing as we visited a little church in a predominantly Amish area out in the country (even more "out in the country" than us!) It was so neat to discover that they have me on their prayer list in their bulletin. I only knew one person in the whole room, but there I was, being remembered in prayer by a bunch of wonderful people I don't even know.

It reminded me that God is with me through this season and His people are, too. I have friends, and family, and people like our new friends at Fairview Baptist Church that we hadn't even met, that are covering us in prayer.

It helps to know this when I am having a "pity party" day. I hate to admit I have those days, but I do. However when I am surrounded by the power of God, and His amazing love, and the kindness and love of so many, those days seem to be a little easier to manage. Thank you for thinking of me, and loving me!

Treatment #3 is this coming Wednesday. I am a little nervous because the last one wiped me out.I have finally been able to exercise a little, and feel much better. Knowing that the cancer is shrinking is worth the uncomfortable part of treatment. Again, would you please join me in prayer for these treatments, that they would do what they are supposed to do? Also please continue to pray for the cure to cancer.

I thank my God upon every remembrance of you, always in every prayer of mine making request for you all with joy... Philippians 1:3-4 NKJV

Blessings

Porch Sittin'

3/20/2010

I love to porch sit! The temperature is warmer, and it feels wonderful to be able to sit on my porch and look at our beautiful valley. Especially sharing it with the ones I love! One of the things that was really important to me when we were looking for a house here was a porch.

Sometimes, if the porch was awesome, I didn't really care what the rest of the house looked like. Well, maybe I did a little! You get the idea though; the porch was VERY important! We also sit on a nice little hill, and the view from our porch can be stunning, no matter what season it is.

We are coming out of a very cold winter, and spring time is beautiful here! The most amazing green colors ever. Everything is blooming, and it is great! Of course, the summer here brings its own beauty, and it is wonderful to sit on the porch and enjoy that season as well, especially after a summer storm.

My favorite season is the fall, we have such a beautiful fall here! Growing up in California, I can't really remember a fall. It just seemed like it went from Summer to a little cooler summer. The trees here are so beautiful. Our valley and the hills around are covered with all different types of hardwood trees, and they are gorgeous in the fall! I can't wait until that time comes each year and we see all the different colors of red, orange and yellow—It is a treat from God. It has been different and beautiful every time! Then there is the winter which brings its own beauty. I love to go out on the porch after a snow and look at the white ground, and how it makes everything seem so clean. Usually can't stay out there for long because it is too cold, but I have to at least take a moment.

So why am I writing about this today? I am just thankful for all God has given me! It is the simplest things in life that we sometimes let slip by. We get caught up in what we are going through, and sometimes lose the ability to enjoy, and love the little things in life, like porch sittin' with someone you love!

Whatever might be happening in your world right

now, take a minute and look at all the wonderful things in your life, even if they seem small. Give thanks to God for those wonderful things, and the things that aren't so wonderful will be easier to handle. God is good, and loves us, me, so much that He gives us little gifts, simple things, to make us smile and remind us that He is truly there with us and watching over us, carrying us!

Nevertheless He did not leave Himself without witness, in that He did good, gave us rain from heaven and fruitful seasons, filling our hearts with food and gladness. Acts 14:17 NKJV

Blessings

Side Effects, Part One-Nausea

3/23/2010

Have you seen those commercials about some great new medicine that sounds as if it's side-effects are worse than the problem it was made to deal with? It makes you wonder who approves this stuff. Chemotherapy can seem like that sometimes. Chemo is some kind of poison cocktail that they shoot into your system to kill cancer cells. What happens, is, it kills all the fast dividing cells in your body, including, but not limited to, those unwanted cancer cells. It also kills a lot of other fast dividing cells, which causes side effects in your body that are both a little unusual and sometimes pretty uncomfortable.

Some folks really suffer with the side-effects of chemo and I would be the last one to make light of that. So many people ask about the side-effects that I thought

I'd write about them for a couple days, because it's something I, unfortunately, have first-hand experience with. If it seems like I'm making light inappropriately, I'm sorry, but I've found that humor really helps me deal with these things while keeping an eye on the Lord and the future.

The first side-effect is nausea. It's not the first in order, necessarily, just the first thing that came to mind. Nausea is that feeling of looming danger deep within your insides that you may, at some very near-future point, lose your cookies. The nausea I experience after chemo is a little different than what I remember as "normal" nausea, like when you've got the flu coming on or something. This feels as if there is a foul tasting, achy, boulder cemented to the insides of my tummy. Eating sounds both horrible and impossible. The thing is I still get hungry. But it feels like anything I swallow would come back up faster than it went down.

Now, the nausea medicine works like crazy, I don't know what people did before they invented this stuff. I hate to imagine it. Thankfully, the nausea hasn't been too bad. It's mostly just a bit yucky for a couple days after chemo then it's okay for a while.

That's enough about nausea, don't you agree?

Blessings

Side Effects, Part Two - Bland Food

3/25/2010

I'm talking about chemotherapy side-effects for a couple days and, having got nausea out of the way first, which is what we all want to do in life, right? Be done with nausea...

The second side-effect is a real bummer for me, especially with the family I married in to and the kids I helped raise. I can no longer eat spicy food! Now, if you know us, you know that we are a family of chili-heads. When we first got married my husband offended me every night when he would soak anything and everything I made with the hottest sauce on the planet. I thought he just didn't like my cooking, when the truth was that his mom, the Queen of Pepper-Heads, raised him to eat spicy food. It didn't take me long to be fully and totally converted, and now I can usually eat just

MaryAnn Goble

about any of the peppers and sauces and zingy goodies that he does and we both love it! Only, presently I cannot do it anymore! One taste of something the slightest bit spicy, and I'm talking like black pepper—and I'm on fire!

One of those areas with fast-dividing cells that the chemo attacks is the digestive system, the saliva, and the whole deal, from tongue, to, well, you know... And spicy food, ANY spicy food, just wipes me out! Not enough saliva to temper the heat. It's so sad because we love to eat spicy food, really love it. So, we both hope this is one side-effect that ends fast, the second this whole ordeal is over.

Because as soon as I can eat spicy food again, we're heading straight to our favorite Mexican-food/ country-karaoke place, for some off-key singing and killer chips and salsa!

Okay, this side-effect isn't so tough to deal with. There are some that are much more of a challenge, but this is real, and if you know Goble's, you can probably feel my pain. I love you!

Blessings

Side Effects, Part Three, Metal Stuff

3/26/2010

I'm taking a few lines here in the blog to write about chemo side-effects. Fun, huh? Nobody likes chemo side-effects, as far as I know. It's not like it gives you any super-hero ability like shooting spider webs out of your wrists. Chemo side-effects, for the most part, are very unpleasant.

Today I'm thinking about a real strange one. But it's funny! I've met quite a few people that have gone through a similar chemo schedule as me, and they all say the same thing—there is a distinct taste of metal in your mouth! And if a bite of food involves metal in any way, like eating off a fork or spoon, or maybe eating something that came out of a can, forget about it. I can't even flip pancakes or wrap leftovers in foil - I go all buggy-eyed and crazy. Is that weird, or what?

So we've had to buy plastic forks and spoons and Ed has to cut all my food for me and flip the eggs and anything else that involves metal stuff. He doesn't mind, but I'm not sure he's buying the whole thing, as it doesn't seem rational, even to me, and I know it's real! But he dutifully deals with all the metal stuff while the hairs on my neck rise up and I taste pennies and nickels and all things metal if I even look at a fork. Blah!

I really hope this side-effect ends asap because I sound crazy when I describe it to people and there are lots of reasons that I might be considered crazy, but this isn't one of them. This is real... At least I think it is...

Then God said, "Look! I have given you every seed-bearing plant throughout the earth and all the fruit trees for your food. Genesis1:29 NLT

Cool, as long as I don't have to use a fork!

Blessings

Side Effects, Part Four, Hair!

3/27/2010

I will end this series of entries on chemo side-effects by talking a bit about the one many people, especially women I think, wonder about the most—hair loss.

Well, it's true, your hair, one of those fast-dividing cells we've talked about, is affected by chemotherapy. But instead of boring you with the details I thought I'd share a poem with you that Ed wrote me a few days after I started noticing a few more strands of hair in my brush than I was used to. Here goes, I hope you enjoy it as much as I have...

Like We Live with A Cat

There is hair in the bathtub,
there is hair in the drain

There is hair by the window,
and some on the pane.

There is hair over here,
there is hair over there.

There is hair on the couch,
on the cushions and chair.

I put on my coat and had hair in a pocket,
I put in a bulb and found hair in the socket.
It's funny at times when you see where it's at,
I kid you not, it's like we live with a cat.

She cut her hair short,
so that if it came loose,

And fell to the floor,
while she rubbed in her mousse,

It would be less severe,
and be less depressing,

Be less of a mess,
to pick off while dressing.

So now we find all these fine little strands,
On the shoulders of sweaters, and the palms of our hands.
Multiplied thousands of course little locks,
On pillows, and plates, in our shoes, on our socks.

The funny part is ,

that it's still hard to tell,

Her head is still hairy,
as if all is still well.

With thick auburn hair,
she could easily cover,

Two sisters, a cousin,
four dogs and a brother.

So we keep the broom handy, and outside the rake,
We carefully pick the hair off of our cake.
We'll sweep and we'll clean and we'll wipe this and that,
And I kid you not, it's like we live with a cat.

I know, I live with a man who loves me unconditionally and makes me laugh! I am very blessed! I hope you have enjoyed this series as much as I have enjoyed sharing it with you. Laughter is good for the soul, and good medicine.

A merry heart does good, like medicine, But a broken spirit dries the bones. Proverbs 17:22 NKJV

Find something to smile about every day!

Blessings

Dreading Chemo
3/29/2010

Have you ever dreaded something? You make an appointment for the dentist, but you really hate going to the dentist, so you begin to think about and dread the day you have to go? I had a history class not long ago and the teacher was a lecturer. He would throw so many dates and facts at us, and his test were just little one word prompts, and we would have to fill in all that information he had given us! I dreaded this, because I knew I would forget everything that he had said! I guess this is how I am feeling today. I will be having chemo treatment #4 this week, and I am dreading it a little. I know that the cancer is shrinking, and so I know the chemo, plus God, is working, but still.

After chemo, I just don't feel great. Actually, I feel like I have been hit by a Mack truck. I don't like to be still for all that long, but my body just can't do much for a few days. My husband and daughter are so great, and patient. They are taking such good care of me, and I feel so blessed by this. My side effects haven't been really severe, and I thank God!

So, what do I do? I just keep praying! I ask the Lord all the time to not only heal me, but help me get through the chemo treatments, and the days following. I have to hold on to Him. He is my strength, and I know He is carrying me! This is true, no matter how I feel, or what I am going through. He will never, ever leave me! He loves me, and wants me to ask Him for His help in everything I do, and am going through. All my circumstances! He wants the same for you too! He loves us so much! He wants to be a part of everything in our life. All He asks of us is to believe. To trust Him, and let Him be in charge! Let Him!

May you know the love of Jesus greater than ever this week!

Blessings

Happy Easter
4/4/2010

It's Easter! It is so beautiful here this morning with all the new life bursting forth all around us! If you live in an area with winter, like we do, I'm sure you agree that those first few weeks of sunshine is one of the greatest feelings in the world! Kelly is coming today to spend a week with us, and I am so excited! I will have my hubby and two of my beautiful daughters with me, what a blessing! I miss my youngest but know that she'll be home soon! She is able to spend this wonderful Sunday with family in California, so I am thankful for that. May we all be reminded that this day is a celebration of life in the Lord! By His resurrection we are able to live. Amen, and Amen! Our life in the Lord is a gift, and we should celebrate it every day.

The joy of the Lord is my strength! I have made it

through four chemo treatments, now am just waiting on the next four to be set up and praying that I will handle those as well as I did the first series. Cancer can't beat me because Jesus is carrying me and He has already won the battle - the victory is His and I am safe and healed in Him! I can do all things through Christ who strengthens me!

I continue to be so thankful for each of you who have committed to love and pray for me and my family through this season! I just wanted to say thank you again, because I have felt so loved and covered in prayer, and it has given me such peace. There is nothing like the peace of my Lord in my life especially in this season. Even when I am not feeling so great, I can feel His arms around me and His gentle voice assuring me that He is with me, and will never let go of me! I have been reminded that there is still much for me to do here on this earth. He is not finished with me yet, and though there has been this bump in the road, what I am experiencing and learning through this is a testimony to His glory and love! He is reminding me that He has made me a strong woman of God! I give Him all the glory and honor because He is worthy!

May this Easter Sunday be filled with remembering our Lord and all that He has done. May y'all have the love of family surrounding you, and the joy that brings! May we never forget to keep our hearts and minds in the Word of God, so we can be consumed by His goodness, and not allow the yuck of this world in!

Happy Easter!

Blessings

The Word of God is Life

4/8/2010

Take to heart all the words I have given you today. Pass them on as a command to your children so they will obey every word of this law. These instructions are not mere words—they are your life! By obeying them you will enjoy a long life in the land you are crossing the Jordan River to occupy. Deuteronomy 32:46-47 NLT

These words were given to Moses to tell the children of Israel. They were a bunch of unfocussed, senseless people, "foolish" as they are called in Deut. 32:28. Why? Because they were choosing to not listen to the Lord, and not obey the commands they had been given. Sound familiar? Every time we choose to not listen, or not hide His Words in our heart, this happens to us as well. We become clueless! God loves us so much, and

desires a relationship with us, and He gives us everything we need, and instructions on how to live in His
Word.

The Bible is as relevant today as it has always been!
The instruction in the verse is to pass these commands
on to our children, and not just pass them on, but tell
them how important it is to follow God and His ways
for our life! God says they are not "mere words", they
are life! We can't live without them! Not only are they
life, but they are healing as well! If we obey them, we
will enjoy a long life! Amen and Amen! I am holding
to that promise! I know that His Word is Healing to
my body and soul! By hiding His Word in our hearts
and living by them, we will be able to occupy whatever
land the Lord sees fit to give us, and through the work
of Jesus, we will live eternally with God the Father, and
Jesus in Heaven!

Thank you, Lord for healing my body and soul.
Thank you for Your Word of life! Thank you that you
have done everything, given everything to have a
relationship with me and anyone else who responds to
Your love! I am focusing on Jesus, My Healer through
this process, and prayerfully considering all that I will
be able to share about His love!

Blessings

Faith
4/14/2010

Well, I don't even know where to begin...I am so thankful to my Lord and Savior! What an amazing God we have! I was given such a good report from the doctors this time, and I can't thank God enough. Let me go back a couple of days...

So, I finished the first set of chemo treatments, four rounds, one every two weeks. I did very well with just mild side effects thanks to Jesus. I have so many people praying for me that I am overwhelmed and blessed! God is listening and answering our prayers. I have had two "med checks" which is where I see the medical oncologist to see the progress we are making.

The first time we were told the cancer was shrinking, and we could tell just by looking that it was, and we praised God. This time we went, and I still felt confident in my healing, and could still tell the cancer is shrinking because of look and feel, but was so relieved when the doctors confirmed this! They not only confirmed it but were really excited about the progress we are making, and told me they felt the cancer could shrink completely, which is something they said would not happen in my case. I was excited by this report! It is hard to put into words, the joy and gratitude, and excitement I feel.

The thing is, from the beginning I knew that God is my Healer and I had nothing to fear. The enemy isn't going to win this one. This disease does not belong in my body, and Jesus is healing me even if it is through medical treatment. I thank Him so much for the doctors He has blessed me with, and pray that I can be a witness to them of His amazing grace! I would not know what to do in this season if I didn't have my faith in God.

My faith and I are old friends. I have had my faith since I was ten years old, which was... well quite a long time ago! God has shown me over and over again throughout my life that He is with me, and will never leave me. These verses are full of power and truth:

Faith is the confidence that what we hope for will actually happen; it gives us assurance about things we

cannot see. Hebrews 11:1 NLT

Confidence that what we hope for will actually happen! I love this! It is happening for me, and others close to me! There is also assurance too, though I cannot see the end of this season, I know God can, and He is with me!

The Lord answered, "If you had faith even as small as a mustard seed, you could say to this mulberry tree, 'May you be uprooted and thrown into the sea,' and it would obey you! Luke 17:6 NLT

Faith in God is powerful! All we need is to know Him, know His Word, walk in Him, obey Him, and have faith that He will never let us go! He loves us so much, and He has done everything to draw us to Him. We just need faith! My prayer is while I am in this season, someone will notice the Lord in me, and have faith that He loves them, and they will give their heart fully and completely to Him!

Amen and Amen!

Blessings

Jesus Can Fix It

4/21/2010

Do you remember when you were little and your favorite toy broke? Nowadays it probably just needs a new battery, but back then things really broke. Whether it was a doll or a bike or a toy truck, there was nothing worse than a world-shattering broken toy. I would try and fix it, but a lot of times would need some help, so my only hope was my dad. He could fix anything! There were times, though, when I "broke it really good" if you know what I mean and dad would just look at me and the toy, and say, "Hmmm, not sure we can fix this one." But he would try, and sometimes the whole ordeal would end with a hug and the assurance that we could get a new one sometime.

Dads are great like that!

Well, our Abba Father in Heaven is the most amazing fixer of all! There is nothing He can't fix! He knows just what to do! These words are so true! The Alabama Spirituals have a song on their new cd that talks about this very thing! It is so refreshing to rest in the assurance that I can take anything to the Lord in prayer. Every broken dream or shattered heart, every wound and every sickness.

Jesus will fix it! God is life, and the maker of our body and soul, and mind and heart. He made us! He will know exactly what to do!

My body has a brokenness inside right now, one that doesn't just make you sad, like a busted toy, but one that can make you very, very sick. Can Jesus even fix this? You bet He can and I am relying on my Maker to restore me to a healthy child of God! I know He's going to fix it for me!

Amen!

Blessings

Another Side Effect?
4/27/2010

Side-effects, yippee! Just about the time you think you've dealt with every possible thing chemotherapy could throw at you, some new, odd, side effect crops up. This time it is the tips of my fingers, nails and all, they have become super-tender, so tender that my wonderful hubby can hold my hands and gently caress them, and it feels like slamming my fingers in a door—very strange, and painful! And the pain is so bad it saps my strength, I can't even open zip-lock baggies or shuffle cards.

We were playing cards with dear friends, John and Patrick, and I had to pass my deal every time because of the pressure it put on my fingertips, geez! It's Wimp City. Then, each of the fingernails is developing a little dark spot, a bruise, right in the center. It's like the bullseye for tenderness, touch that and I'm going into orbit...

Then there's the rash... That's never good, right? I got some new hand lotion that sounded too good to be true, and guess what? It was! The tops of my hands are now covered in an itchy, bumpy rash - just because of some sneaky ingredient in the lotion that the chemo drug decided to pick a fight with. So, my hands are sore AND itchy. Are we having fun yet?

Well, all this will end with the chemo treatments, though, and I've completed five out of eight, so we're almost there! My side-effects have been mild compared to what I hear others have gone through and I'm humbly grateful to God for that. Ed says mine are just as bad as others, it's just that I'm one tough redhead, I don't know about that, but I do know that I am ever grateful to the Lord for carrying me through all this. I'm willing to deal with these uncomfortable irritations because the end result will be healing. It's like the bible says about "our light affliction" that we deal with as believers in this life, it all leads to the marvelous, wonderful life prepared for us in Christ.

I have so much to be thankful for! My husband, my family, my friends, and most of all God Who loves me more than I can even understand! Amen!

Blessings

Reflection

5/3/2010

Sometimes we blast through life without taking the time to really look where we are going or what we are really doing. When I was a little girl, I knew I wanted to serve the Lord, finish school, meet a man, fall in love, get married, have babies and have a house with a porch and white rockers. It's The American Dream, or my dream, at least. Sometimes we get so caught up pursuing 'stuff' that, as life begins to take shape, we don't realize how great the journey is. It's hard, but it's great!

We forget to thank God for our spouse, or when we were able to buy a house. Pretty soon many of us get in a robotic routine of life: In the car at 7:30, drives kids to school, go to work, pick kids up, go to a practice, home for supper, homework and it's off to bed. The next morning, we start all over agthrough. I would really love to have inspiring words to write to today, but I don't. I am so thankful to my God for knowing me, and loving me right where I am! He knows my heart, and how much I love and trust Him... but He also knows how I really feel! And, wow, I am thankful He loves me anyway!

Blessings

Thanking God In Spite
of My Circumstances

5/7/2010

Well, yesterday I had Chemo #6 and, thank God, made it through... I fully believe in my healing in Jesus' Name, but as much as I know this, chemo is still a hard thing to go through. I would really love to have inspiring words to write to today, but I don't. I am so thankful to my God for knowing me, and loving me right where I am! He knows my heart, and how much I love and trust Him... but He also knows how I really feel! And, wow, I am thankful He loves me anyway!

Today I am tired, my mind isn't working quite right and I feel weak. I should probably go take a nap or something... Isn't that what we tell our kids when they are not being themselves? I think I'll take my own motherly advice... For now, then, let me just say thank you for praying for me and loving me even when I am not so loveable...

I hope that all the moms in my life have a really bless-ed Mother's Day! You all are heroes in my mind, and life!

Blessings

The Greatest Of These Is Love (Part 1)
5/20/2010

And now abide faith, hope, love, these three; but the greatest of these is love. 1 Corinthians 13:13 NKJV

When the Christian life is boiled down to its purest form, what remains is faith, hope and love, and of those, love is the main thing. I think people believe that, for the most part, but we sure have distorted love in our generation to the point where you wonder if people even know what love really is.

In relationships, people sometimes use the "L _ _ _" word just to get what they want, which is usually the "S _ _" word. Oh, how that dishonors the true meaning of love and, actually, reminds me of two more "S" words: stupid and selfish!

There is so much more to love, and when we understand it better, our friendships, our marriages and our families can be full of real love and grow continually closer to God's heart and destiny for our lives. Our relationship with people should be a reflection of God's relationship with us. Of course, understanding the depth of His love toward us in Christ is something we could never fully fathom, being unfailing, full of grace and eternal, but knowing Him more will help our relationships at least move in His direction - not the direction of the world.

We are so selfish that all we seem to worry about is our own comfort and pleasure. And we wonder why so many marriages crash and burn - at the core is a selfish, 'what's in it for me' type of love.

Kind of an "I'll love you if…" When the truth is that there are no "if's" in love. God loves unconditionally, most of us Christians believe that, yet we are quick to put conditions on our own love. Hmmm, something wrong with that picture…

I'm thinking a lot about love during this journey because I realize now more than ever that life is fragile and wasting time following the ways of the world is a trap from the enemy and I'm not playing that game anymore. My eyes are open, and I hope yours are too. Life is short—love God and love people.

Blessings

The Greatest Of These Is Love (Part 2)

5/21/2010

Love bears up under anything and everything that comes, is ever ready to believe the best of every person, its hopes are fadeless under all circumstances, and it endures everything [without weakening]. I Corinthians 13:7 AMP

"Love bears up under anything and everything that comes." Isn't that awesome? Have you ever felt like that? Like "anything and everything" were coming at you? The first response is usually not to bear up under it, but rather to get out from under it and split! Our defense mechanisms aren't used to 'bearing up', they're more inclined to run for cover, run for safety. I guess that's natural, but love means sticking it out sometimes even when it seems all hell is breaking loose on us. We have God's Word and His promises and in Christ we can

God Crushed Cancer

stand against the devices of the enemy and his plan to destroy us and our relationships. God's love will help us "bear up" under anything! Amen!

We're like the toddler who scatters toys all over the room because nothing holds his attention for more than a minute. If he can't figure out how to get the little square piece into the little round hole, forget it, he's moving on to the next toy, that one's broke, it doesn't work, it's not making me happy. Next. We can give up on people like that too if they're not making us happy, not fulfilling our "if" like we talked about before, where, "I'll love you unconditionally, if…"

There is another verse in the Bible that says:

Greater love has no one than this, than to lay down one's life for his friends. John 15:13 NKJV

Laying down your life is something you do. It's an action. A very extreme action, in a literal sense, but an action. It could also mean laying down your plans, comfort, finances or something else, on behalf of someone you love since our 'life' is composed of all those aspects and a million more. The great thing is, when we are sharing pure, selfless love, the love that is returned to us is amazing! I have been blessed to have the kind of love from my husband that is selfless. He's been laying his life down for me for over 30 years. And I've tried to

97

do the same. And it's made our relationship very, very special.

One of the saddest things I have heard on this journey is the story of men who have walked out on their wife after the breast cancer diagnosis. How does that show love? What it shows, is that those men were not thinking of their wives, but thinking of themselves, and not enduring through circumstances that are tough, not *"bearing up under anything and everything."* They are acting like the toddler looking for a toy that isn't broke. This makes me so angry! I can't imagine how hard it must be for these women to face something like cancer all alone. It's scary enough when you are not alone! I am very blessed to have my husband by my side, and he tells me every day that he loves me, and will always be here, and that I am his one and only! Not only that, but he also tells me that I become more beautiful every day!

I guess the bottom line is that we all need to be doing a lot more "bearing up" and a lot less living for ourselves. A lot more loving with God's unfailing love and giving my life for others.

God's love is so deep for us. I want to keep moving closer to Him, and pray my love for others looks more like His, and less like the worlds.

Blessings

There Is Definitely A God

5/24/2010

Today I was thinking about all the people who doubt God's existence. I know the enemy is smart, and tries to keep people in the dark. It is hard to understand sometimes though, because if we really look, we can see God in everything! I was reading my devotion and came across this verse in the Bible about sand...

Do you not fear and reverence Me? says the Lord. Do you not tremble before Me? I placed the sand for the boundary of the sea, a perpetual barrier beyond which it cannot pass and by an everlasting ordinance beyond which it cannot go? And though the waves of the sea toss and shake themselves, yet they cannot prevail [against the feeble grains of sand which God has ordained by nature to be sufficient for His pur-

**pose]; though [the billows] roar, yet they cannot pass
over that [barrier]. [Is not such a God to be reverently
feared and worshiped?] Jeremiah 5:22 AMP**

God formed each grain of sand and piles them together to form a barrier to keep the ocean from moving
over the land. Israel was being warned that punish-
ment was coming, and to confirm that He was able, He
mentioned the image of the sand. A tiny grain of sand
can drive you crazy if it gets stuck in your sandal, but
I'd never really thought about the fact that God uses
them, in mass, to restrain the ocean - wow! And it is an
"everlasting ordinance" so it will never change! What
an image and demonstration of the awesome power
and love of God.

I think people are happiest when they are doing what
they were created to do! Like the sand that is ordained
by God to hold back the sea, people are designed to re-
flect His love in the world and bring God glory through
the conduct of our lives. When we surrender to His
purposes we are most happy! Surrendering is something we keep learning our whole lives. I want to surrender completely to Him, love people unconditionally,
and point them to the Savior I know, He is My Healer!

Blessings

Chemo #7

5/28/2010

Well, Chemo #7 is behind me now— the med-tubes were disconnected and I got out of the chair yesterday afternoon and was chauffeured home by Danece and Melissa just in time to take a nice nap. If this treatment is like the others, I can expect to feel pretty crummy for the next week or so and then I'll start to bounce back. What a process.

The thing that I hold on to in these first days after chemo is that I have a faithful God who has been with me every step of the way and will continue to carry me through to healing and victory! Amen! Also, I hang on to my husband and girls who take care of my every need. And then Kelly and 'my boys' out in California who video chat with me and call with the play-by-play of their games and pray for me as well! I wouldn't know what to do without my family.

I also have a special cousin who talks me through stuff and stands with me in prayer - I want to thank her as well - "Thank you Terilyn!"

I am down to one more treatment. One more chemo before my eyelashes and hair grow back - Yes! I can't wait to see what color and texture it will be, I've been told that can change after chemo, and I've always had thick, course hair, so we'll see!

Thanks for praying for me for the next few days, it kind of feels like a bad flu with lots of aches, only without the frequent trips to the restroom, if that makes any sense. I'll be happy when it's over. I love you!

Blessings

Who I Am
6/1/2010

What do you want to be when you grow up? As for me, I always wanted to be a wife and a mommy. Later, I realized that I also wanted to be an amazing grandma to lots of beautiful grandkids and the apple of God's eye. I want to hear "Well Done!" when I stand before Him someday.

So many of my dreams have come true, God has blessed me with so much and I am realizing more each day as I write these entries that even through my journey with cancer He is changing me and working in me to create a vessel of honor.

The past season of my life was a very selfish time and I want to move as far away from that as I can! The enemy likes keeping people so self-focused that they can't see past themselves, can't see what they are really doing and how they are hurting themselves and others. I just want to run from selfishness and pride, escape all the enemies plans to destroy, and stay close to Jesus' side, listen intently for His whisper of love to my mind and heart. To do this I need to stay close to Him, stay close to godly people, stay in fellowship with the Spirit through the Word and Worship. I need to press in and seek Him with my whole heart, and I am!

God is helping me to see who I am in Him. I realize that I am becoming the woman I dreamed to be, and my dream has been made complete in Him! I'm not perfect, far from it, but my past is forgiven, my future is secure, and my present is covered and protected by my Lord and Savior. There is cancer in my body, although it is about dead by now, but I'm not primarily a "Cancer Patient" or "Cancer Survivor". I am, first and foremost, a child of God, then a wife, mother, grandmother and friend. I am more than a conqueror through Him who loved me and gave His life for me! I am healed, body, mind and spirit! I am a woman of destiny and my destiny is sure!

Oh, how I pray that you, too, can discover who you are—who you really are. And if you find that you are not in Christ, that you are still living under the veil of selfishness and shame, that you drop everything and seek God until you find the peace that passes all understanding and discover your true identity in Christ Jesus!

Blessings

Peace

6/7/2010

"True peace is available only in knowing Christ intimately. All that He said, did, and does is to bring peace in our hearts. He was born to bring it, He taught to explain it. He died on the cross to establish it. He rose from the dead to defeat all the enemies that rob us of it; and He is with each of us now to give... the gift. It pervades our hearts when we put Him first in our lives." Lloyd Ogilvie[1]

Peace... *"pervades our hearts when we put Him first..."* I often wonder what people do that don't know the Lord. They are missing this amazing peace that knowing Him brings. Plus we have the peace of knowing that our lives in Him are secure in this life and also

---

1   Lloyd John Ogilve, God's Best for My Life

after we leave this world. We have the peace that we will live with Him forever. Along with the peace that knowing Christ brings is the peace that we have when we "know all is well" as someone said to me earlier this week. When we are walking with the Lord, and striving to please Him, we are trying to do and be where we are supposed to be. That brings amazing peace! Resting in the Lord, and knowing that we are trying to do what is right brings peace to our lives and hearts, and that is priceless.

The enemy tries so hard to steal and destroy, and he tries to take us down that path with him. He lies and tries to influence us to make selfish choices which always end in confusion - and where there is confusion there can be no peace.

Holding onto the Lord and walking with Him is where I want to be. I need His peace in my life. Our God is amazing, and wise. He offers this amazing peace to us, because He loves us and want us to be whole and complete. Sickness can bring uncertainty like a tornado cloud on the horizon, but Jesus offers peace in the midst of any storm and I rest on His promises every moment of the day.

You can have the peace of Jesus, the peace that passes all understanding, if you will walk in His ways and obey His commands, even as Jesus instructed us to.

The resulting victory and joy in life is wonderful! I am so thankful for my country, my home, my husband and my family and friends, they all bring me peace in many ways, but the peace of Jesus is what really gets me through the night.

Blessings

Make Every Moment Count

6/14/2010

We have all heard this, and probably said it a million times. It is so easy to let "moments" slip by us, and then wonder; "Where did the time go?" We spend our moments working, sleeping, eating, and a gazillion other ways. I wonder how I can truly make every moment count. I know from life experience that some things that take up our moments should be put aside, and those precious moments should be shared with our loved ones. I remember as a young mom, telling my girls "hold on, mommy is busy right now." I know that sometimes this couldn't be helped, but I also know that I could have done the dishes later and played dolls with my girls. I could have vacuumed another day, and spent the time with my wonderful, amazing husband. I have spent moments in anger and said things that I wish I could take back, messing up that precious moment...You get the picture.

We waste a lot of moments. The sad thing is, once the moment has passed, it is gone. My husband has said: "Our relationships are the most important thing in this life!" Those words are so true! We have heard about the dad that works so much, his kids don't expect him to come to anything... dance recital, ball game, track meet. The impression this leaves on the child is that dad wasn't around much. He missed that precious moment with his kids! Moments are so PRECIOUS!

When you hear the word "cancer", you think about your time (moments) a little more. I know I have. I know my "moments" on this earth are not done! I still have much to do! The Lord is healing me of this cancer so I can have many, many more moments! I am so honored and thankful to Him! I want so much to choose to make my moments count for me and my loved ones! I want to spend those precious moments with the Lord, listening to what He wants for me. I want to honor Him in my moments!

Let's not the miss the opportunities we have to share our love! Let's not miss the opportunity to share His love! It is so much more important to leave this world having touched the lives of people. Hopefully they will remember what kind of person we were! Let's truly "Make Every Moment Count!"

Blessings

Chemo #8

6/16/2010

Well, tomorrow is the last chemo...I know it is my last chemo! I know that through this process the Lord is healing me! The time has passed so quickly. God is amazing, and I have been humbled to see Him protect me, and carry me, and love me. I have not experienced rough side effects like many people do. I have had days of not feeling good, well actually feeling pretty bad, but He has helped me each step of the way.

The next step is clear, I am going to have surgery in the next couple of months and then radiation. I am a little hesitant but know that the process of my healing will be complete when this is finished. I am trusting in the Lord and holding His hand. There is no better place to be! The insurance we have is changing, and this brings some issues that I am concerned about. But, I know the Lord will take care of everything! He hasn't brought me this far to stop now! He will complete the work He has begun in me... Just as God took care of Elijah and the people he was with, in I Kings

17, I know, that I know, that I know, He will carry me through until all the cancer is gone! In Jesus Name Amen!

Thank you to all who have been praying. I certainly have been able to feel your love and friendship. I am blessed to have y'all part of my life and thinking of me!

I will keep y'all updated on the next step and covet your continued prayers!

Blessings

Angry!
6/22/2010

I have had my last chemo! I know it is my last one! I am assured of my healing in Jesus Name! This one seems to be harder on me... Maybe it is because I am expecting to feel completely better, I don't know exactly. I just know I am REALLY sore! I know it will pass and am thankful that it is just a little pain.

Feeling a little angry today! About having cancer, and how I hurt, and can't do all the things I want to for my family. Hating that they hurt for me and don't really know what to do for me. Also, just angry because I don't want this anymore, never wanted it! I am also angry because I have friends and family who have had this, and some still dealing with it and I just want to scream! NO ONE should ever have to go through this! It is devastating, and painful, and emotional! It makes me angry that because of sin, sickness is in this world! I know the Lord knows I am angry, so I guess I just wanted to vocalize it! I remember having a discussion one time with someone in a Bible study about how Christians should never get angry. I don't believe this. We should never get angry and sin, but I believe God made us just the way we are. He gave us everything, including our emotions. Remember when Jesus got angry and threw the guys out of the temple? Hopefully if this emotion surfaces, it causes us to get off of our butts and do something to change things and make a positive difference!

I saw a GodTube story today about a very young man diagnosed with colon cancer. He had a wife and 3 children, and eventually died from this disease... This makes me so angry! Cancer is awful, and people die from it every day. However, this man's story was so full of hope and amazing faith in Jesus! Though he has left this life, he has begun a new life in heaven with our Savior. His family is hurting though. It is hard to lose someone! Even when we know the Lord, we grieve for people when they leave us. The enemy wants us to believe there is no hope, especially with the diagnosis of cancer. NOT TRUE! There is ALWAYS hope! We need to continue to pray for the cure to this awful disease! People close to me have cancer like me and are some of the strongest people I know! Some have survived, and some are still dealing with it, but all have shown me how to be strong, courageous, unwavering in my faith! These people are my heroes!

We can complain about a lot of things sometimes, but why? I am convinced if we wake up each day, thank the Lord for our breath, family, home, etc... Our day would look brighter! If we would allow God to work fully in us, and let Him be God, and not try and take His place, life would be easier and so much more fulfilling! I know that He ALWAYS has my good in mind, and He has your good in mind! The fact that He wants the best for everyone should help me understand just WHO He is, and let Him be God!

Just blowing off a little steam and trying to be who God wants me to be everyday, in every situation.

Blessings

Happy 4th of July!

7/4/2010

Our little town celebrated the "4th" on the "3rd" this year and we had a great day of enjoying the festivities topped off by a beautiful fireworks show. I really enjoyed it! The city park was full of people playing 'corn-hole' and eating funnel cakes. It was fun to people watch and hang out with family while waiting for the fireworks to start! Of course, none of this would be possible if not for all the men and women who have secured our freedom over the years through the American Armed Forces! I have had many family members and friends who have served in the military, and I am so thankful for them. We have much to be thankful for in our country! God bless America!

Our God is still in control of everything, even when it appears things are going completely down the drain.

MaryAnn Goble

This is true in our country and in our personal lives. My life for the past few months has been challenging, to say the least. My hope has always been, and will always be in my God, and the fact that He is my Healer! I always have the love of my family and friends as well. I am so thankful for all the freedoms we have, especially the freedom to worship and serve the Lord.

I am scheduled for surgery, and know this is moving toward completing the healing that the Lord has begun in me! Yes, I am a little concerned about all this entails, but I trust Him! I trust my husband and family to be here for me, and I have many friends I trust to pray, and be here when they can. I am a very lucky woman!

My prayer today is that we all will remember to be thankful for our God, our country, our armed forces, our families and friends! Being thankful is a good way to celebrate our Independence!

Blessings

Trust
7/8/2010

Trust is the confident expectation of something; hope; reliance on the integrity, strength, ability, surety, etc., of a person or thing; confidence. to expect confidently; hope.[2]

It is so important to have trust in our lives. It is very important for us to be trustworthy. I trust people. I think the best of people, because I want them to be trustworthy. This isn't always the case, but that is how I choose to view people until otherwise proven. Most importantly, I trust in God. He has never, ever let me down. He is always Who He says He is. Over and over again, He has proven to me that I can rely on Him, and He will never change. He is the same yesterday, today, and forever! He says He is my Healer, and I believe this with all that is in me! I know I am healed in Jesus

2   *Webster's Dictionary*

Name!

So many of the challenges we face today happen because we don't trust anymore. We also have become people who don't always keep our word. We say things and do something else. or promise something, and then not do it. Wouldn't this world be a nicer place if we would just keep our word? Trust in God first, be someone whom others can trust, and then expect the best from people. If we are trustworthy, it helps others to want to be the same.

I know I have failed in this area sometimes. I am moving forward trying to be a better person, someone whom others can trust in! I want to be the person I profess to be. I want people to look at me and see Jesus! We can trust in Him!

Blessings

Honesty

7/9/2010

The word honest is defined as honorable in principles, intentions, and actions; upright and fair, genuine or unadulterated.[3]

Honesty is a trait that seems to be less noticeable these days... while other traits or characteristics seem to be overflowing from the depths of who we are. This is so sad. Do you remember the days when a handshake was all that was needed to seal a deal with someone? The days when "your word was your bond?" I think the trouble begins with us not being honest with ourselves. This leads to not being honest with others. From there it is a downhill road. How are we not honest with ourselves? By not seeing the need for a Savior. Thinking we have no need for God in our lives.

3   *Webster's Dictionary*

Feeling powerful enough to take care of ourselves, in every situation. There are so many who are convinced they have no need for Jesus. Even as Christians, we often times try to do things, fix things, with our own strength. Saying to ourselves and to the Lord; "I've got this." If we were being truly honest, we would be able to see our need for help every day. Especially from the Lord, but certainly from others as well.

Today people are driven by power, the need to be self-sufficient, to have everything, and have it "our way." This leads to many, many broken and dishonest people. In the book; "In The Name Of Jesus," by Henri J. M. Nouwen, the author states: *"Beneath all the great accomplishments of our time there is a deep current of despair. While efficiency and control are the great aspirations of our society, the loneliness, isolation, lack of friendship and intimacy, broken relationships, boredom, feelings of emptiness and depression, and deep sense of uselessness fill the hearts of millions of people in our success-oriented world."* So while suggesting all we need is "efficiency and control", we are not honest about what deep needs are within us.

If we were truly a honest people, we would see our need for Jesus, a relationship with Him. We would understand that we need His love. We would also understand that in the deepest part of us, what we want most, is to be loved by others. A true love, not the false one that is portrayed in this world today.

I want to go before the Lord every day, and pour myself out before Him. Being completely honest with Him. Then I will know that I am going in the right direction. I want to love others more than judge them. I want others to see in me the honesty that I want to see in them. I want to show them unconditional love, so they can see Jesus in me.

I am in a season that I feel the need to be completely honest and learn how to do that in every season to come. In honesty, I have been confident and afraid, angry and humbled. However, what really matters is my ability to trust in the Lord. To be honest with Him about all I am feeling.

Honestly, I know I am healed in Jesus Name! I know He is with me through this trial.

Oh that we all would be completely honest with ourselves and the Lord. Then find people we trust to be completely honest with them, and keep ourselves accountable.

Blessings

What Is Peace?

7/11/2010

Harmony in personal relations, freedom from disquieting or oppressive thoughts or emotions, a state of tranquility or quiet? All of these are part of peace. All of which we can have when we surrender to Jesus. Give Him all that we have, and allow Him to work in us. There is nothing more amazing than to walk and feel secure in the peace that comes from Jesus. I have experienced this peace over and over again in my life, but especially in the past few months. Even in the midst of a huge trial, we can have the peace that Jesus gives. I know first-hand. When the word cancer was spoken concerning me, I was frightened. However, taking this illness to the Lord, and leaving it at His feet, has allowed me to walk through this healing process with an amazing amount of peace! Yes, there have been times that I hurt, and I could tell there was a war going on in my body. Even during those times, I have been over-whelmed with His peace. You see, I have been walking with the Lord for a while now, and I trust Him. I also have experienced this peace so many times, and am assured that He never changes, and always wants what is best for me. He has proven Himself to me, not that He needed to. He has shown me He is faithful and always does what He says He will. How could I not have peace even in this storm?

I love Him. I trust Him. I know resting in Him brings me peace. My body needs this peace right now, and so I am going to the Source!

Blessings

The Gift of Life
7/13/2010

It is so much fun to give and receive gifts on a birthday or Christmas or even for no reason at all except as a gesture of love! One of the best gifts of all is LIFE! And that life is found in Jesus. He said, "I have come that they might have life, and have it more abundantly." Every day we wake up to a new morning, a new opportunity, we are given an abundant gift from the Lord. Looking at life this way can make all the difference.

When we see life as special, and precious, we are more likely to do more with it, and give more away. If we choose to be all that we can, and give all that we can, life is amazing. When something happens, such as cancer, or any life-threatening illness, we take inventory of our lives and covenant to live better; be a better person; to bless our families and friends. We tend to realize, especially if we didn't before, that we will not live on this earth forever. The reality is we should do this all the time. Live every day to its fullest, because we are not promised tomorrow. Treat everyone in the best possible way, love them unconditionally. We are not going to be remembered for our "things", but our relationships.

Take the time to meet Jesus, and accept His gift of life, and give Him everything we are, so we can live right now to praise Him and honor Him! He makes our time here full and truly abundant!

Blessings

Thankful AGAIN!

7/26/2010

Okay, so today I am wishing all was finished. I feel like I have been dealing with this FOREVER, even though I was first diagnosed only about seven months ago, while many people I know have been battling cancer of one flavor or another for years. It is so amazing to me how God has shown Himself to me, reminding me daily how much He loves me, and how He is holding me in His hands!

I was reminded again that He is with me when I received a letter from my surgeon in the mail. The "Amazing Dr. Chagpar", as Ed calls her, is the Director of the Breast Program at the renown Brown Cancer Center, an incredible professional at the cutting edge of her field. The very fact that I was able to have her as my surgeon was a gift from God. It all happened so quickly, from my diagnosis, by a Doctor who didn't know me from Eve, the subsequent strings he pulled to get me into Dr. Chagpar's office, and her taking my case. She has managed my care and this past week conducted my surgery.

Well, the letter I mentioned was sent to inform me (and all of her patients I'm sure) that Dr. Chagpar was relocating, assuming a high-level position in another part of the country. What a blessing that, just as we are finishing, she would be moving. It could have been a month ago, or two weeks ago, I guess, but it wasn't. My surgery was able to be performed by this woman who I have grown to trust with my care. Thank you, Lord!

I pray that as Dr. Chagpar moves on, that her research will help to find the cure to this type of cancer. I am so humbled and thankful that I was allowed to be her patient.

I am doing really well. I am looking forward to seeing my surgeon one more time, next week, and thank her and encourage all that she is doing for folks like me. I am also so thankful to my Father in Heaven, who continues to show me that I am loved by Him, and nothing is a surprise to Him concerning me (or you). Life is a bumpy road, but God is there, every step of the way, going before us and preparing things beforehand, that we might walk in them.

Blessings

Happy Saturday!
8/7/2010

I am doing well! I know that Jesus is with me through this whole process and He is my Healer! I continue to get good reports from the doctors.

My youngest daughter Melissa went back to college yesterday to finish her Senior year. It is hard to believe, and we are so proud of her! I am so excited for her to be able to be there (CA). Hopefully when I get the okay, we will take a road trip to see her and my oldest daughter, Kelly, and her family! I am glad that they are at least in driving distance from each other so they can have sister time. Danece is staying here with me probably until October. I am blessed so much by these beautiful daughters of mine, and their love for the Lord and each other, and Ed and I!

Please continue to pray for my friend Kim. She is battling cancer and it has become very hard for her. She knows the Lord and is a fighter! Please pray with me for healing for her, and strength to continue to fight this disease. It can be so overwhelming. God is Big and sees ALL of our needs! Amen!

My prayer for all y'all is that you have a very blessed and Happy Saturday!

Blessings

It's Raining!

8/18/2010

Today I woke up to the sound of rain outside which usually, around here, means it is going to become cooler. We have been having record heat the past couple of weeks, so cooler temperatures will be a welcome change. Just about the time I thought the heat was unbearable it begins to change. Nice!

I am reminded once again of words from a very wise man (my hubby) who wrote in his book, Sincerely, Jesus, *"Jesus defines the limits of your trial, not Satan. Jesus said they would have tribulation for ten days. Not eleven, not twelve. No matter how long Satan would like to prolong it, it doesn't matter, Jesus set's the boundary, and He said TEN Days - you can make it! You can do anything for ten days!"*

When I began to look at my life as a season of time like this, it helped me to hold on. Just when I thought I might not be able to handle something for much longer, or even felt near to the end of my rope, the season changed, and it was over, I reached "day ten" so to speak. This past season, which has lasted pretty much all of 2010 so far, has been a little stormy, but the storms are subsiding, and I am reminded that my God is MUCH bigger than the storm. He said I could make it ten days, and I made it!

My prayer today is for the people I know, and also those I don't, that are in the "stormy" season of cancer, or any illness. Jesus, please send Your Healing Rain to cleanse our bodies of all illness, and refresh our souls. We need Him in every season of life, and remember that He alone knows all of our needs. Jesus loves you and you can make it through this season.

Blessings,

Beauty

9/2/2010

As women, and I am sure it is true with men as well, we want to look the most beautiful for the special people in our lives. The thing is, being the most beautiful to people really starts on the inside. Oh, I am the first to admit that I care what I look like on the outside. I am not ready to have any gray hair, so I give a lady some money to make it a different color! That seems silly sometimes to me, but I do. We spend time trying to decide what to wear in the mornings, to look our best for the day. I put make-up on to feel better about myself, though my husband would say I don't need any... I try and exercise every day to keep this body of mine in shape, even as it gets older. We all do things to make ourselves look better on the outside. There is really nothing wrong with doing things to make us look better on the outside, though some spend way too much time thinking about this, and not working on the person they are supposed to be.

Being a beautiful person requires inner beauty. We were probably told as children that we need to be kind, sweet, polite, caring, respectful. Others like when a person has these qualities, this is inner beauty. Of course, the most important part of inner beauty is knowing the Lord. When we allow Him to work in our lives and mold us into the person He wants us to be, including the qualities mentioned above, we are beautiful inside and out. In His eyes, we are beautiful from the beginning of our lives. He loved us so much, thought so much of us, that He was willing to die for us. WOW!

This past year has been a tough one for me as far as my outer appearance goes. My family would say that I haven't changed a bit, because to them I am still beautiful. However, as a cancer survivor (AMEN!), I have had moments of not looking my best on the outside... As a woman, having eyelashes is kind of important! Seeing pictures of myself in the hospital was almost more than I could take, because it didn't seem to look like me. Yet, I told my daughter I wanted lots of pictures because I want to have a visual record of this season of my life. Women all over the world have to endure what this disease does to their outer appearance. We feel bad, we are hard on ourselves because we can't seem to look our best when we feel like we have been hit by a truck. What I have been reminded of through this experience, and throughout my life, it's the inner beauty that counts the most! I want to be beautiful to the Lord first, then allow Him to shine out of my life, and maybe my countenance will show His beauty to others.

You know, the women and men I have met that are facing, or have faced this disease, are the most beautiful people in the world! They are enduring an illness that is devastating yet doing it with grace and strength! Fighting for your life tends to put things into perspective and concentrating on our inner person and having inner beauty becomes so much more important than our outer appearance. Pleasing the Lord and wanting Him to shine His beauty out of us is so much more effective than any makeup or hair color, or even any weight loss program! Wouldn't it be wonderful if we all would think about the inside much more than the outside, before an illness takes us there?

Blessings

He Is Thinking About Me!
9/15/2010

This morning I woke up in awe of the Lord. I hope I do this every morning, but this morning in particular God was impressing on me that He was thinking of me, that is, not only was I thinking about Him at that moment, but He was thinking about me! Can you imagine that? Along with holding the world together and keeping the oceans inside of their boundaries, and a zillion other things and other people, He has you and I in mind right now, personally. That's too much to comprehend, really.

Then I was overwhelmed by the selfishness of mankind. It's so frustrating. Most of the trouble we get into is because we are so self-seeking. As Christians we are supposed to be looking more and more like Jesus every day, and HE is the antithesis of selfish. If, for one moment, we could take our eyes off of ourselves and focus solely on others, THAT would be more like Jesus, and a good start toward being who He has called us to be.

Putting others before ourselves brings us joy, and we are happier when we do this. Why is it that we can't seem to get this through our thick heads? I think if we could do this, "we", starting with myself, first, could change the world—we really could. Jesus put others first, put His Father first, primarily, and He absolutely changed the world for all time. Like Sheldon[4] wrote, we should follow "in his steps."

It has been a hard year for "me." The truth is, it has been a hard year for many people. My illness was hard on my family, not just me...So, while I could choose to have a pity party, I hope that I can rise above this.I don't want to focus just on me. I want to use every circumstance I have gone through to be a blessing! I am ready to have the focus off of me and look for others to focus on and pour love, kindness, excitement for life into, and share the Mightiness of God! My prayer is that I might be able to encourage others who are facing illness and let them know that God is thinking of them, He hasn't left them, and He loves them very much!

I am so thankful that God is thinking of you and me - right now!

Blessings

---

4 Charles Sheldon, In His Steps, pub. 1896

Just Thinking...

10/11/2010

When I think of all I have been through this past year, I can hardly believe it is almost over...I had my last radiation treatment this past week! I will still have follow-up doctor appointments and such, but I am so grateful to God for holding me through this journey. My family has been amazing and continues to show me how much they love and appreciate me. I am thankful to so many friends that have shared thoughts and prayers with me, and just let me know they were thinking of me.

Though my body has had to endure much, my soul has been renewed .Even those days when I just didn't feel like doing anything, God showed up and told me He was there, and I/We WOULD get through this! He only speaks truth, and He promised to never leave us or forsake us.I have been reminded of this over and over.

When it feels like you are all alone, or like no one is listening, or understands, and you just wanna give up, please don't, God loves you so much and you are precious to Him, and He always has your best in mind! HE will never leave you, He will demonstrate His love and faithfulness in amazing, unexpected ways throughout whatever journey you find yourself on.

Thank y'all so much for loving on me and my family, and praying for me! I can't say thank you enough...

Blessings

The Gift

12/26/2010

As Christians, we celebrate Jesus' birthday on Christmas. He is the best gift of all. God loved us so much, and knew we needed help to live the Life that He so generously wanted us to have, so He gave His best in His Son. Of course, when we accept His Son, we also get the benefit of eternal life. This in itself is quite extraordinary! However, there is so much more...

The Love that God has for us and gives us so freely is amazing! When we allow ourselves to rest in His arms, and follow His way, and release EVERYTHING to Him, we begin to experience how much He loves us. Yes, He desired us to be able to live with Him forever, but He also desires for us to have a full life here. Now that word, "full" can mean a lot of things. I am thinking of the kind of "full" that we experience sometimes when all the food spread before us at the holiday dinner table somehow manages to enter our bodies. We tell ourselves there is no more room, but we keep grazing. You know the best part about being "full" of the Lord? He keeps putting more in! As long as we are willing, empty vessels, He will put more in. He never runs out of blessing for us. He will fill our lives with peace, hope, love, mercy, grace. He has given us ALL that we need to fill our life to overflowing. The idea is if we are overflowing, we will have much to share with those around us.

Giving of ourselves to others is awesome and full of blessing.

As this year comes to a close for myself and my family, with all the hurting and sickness, there is still much to look back and be thankful for. God, Who holds onto me. My amazing husband that continues to show me I am loved deeply by him. My daughters who are amazing, funny, and full of the Lord! My son-in-law who I continue to see growing in the Lord. My grandsons whom I love, and enjoy doing so many wonderful things with. They amaze me every time we are together! I have had an amazing journey this year, and though it was tough, I was reminded again and again that God will NEVER leave me or forsake me! As the New Year approaches, I hope I daily see the blessing of being His child! I will wake up EVERYDAY thanking

Him for healing my body, my heart when it was hurting, my soul so I can see how to help others. I will carry the spirit of giving into every moment!

This life can be so "full" if I just remember to empty myself...

Blessings to all of you this New Year.

Sitting In His Lap

12/29/2010

I wrote this not long ago, and my hubby said I should post it as a blog. I know sometimes I am praying and am overwhelmed by the amazing love of My Heavenly Father! This was one of those times. I know that I can go to Him no matter what. As I was praying, I was just amazed by His desire to want to hold me, shelter me, wipe my tears. He LOVES me. Wow! My prayer is that somehow you are blessed from my thoughts.

When I am on my knees, broken by all the wrong I have done, and I realize how much I have hurt the One Who loves me most, sometimes I want to hide. In that quiet moment I realize His presence shelters me, surrounds me, protects me. I hear His voice as quiet as a whisper telling me: *"I AM is here, right here with you, and I know you. The LOVE I have for you will never change.*

You are safe to be you, and know that I AM is working in you to mold you, complete you. Crawl up into My lap, let Me hold you."

I am overwhelmed by love, and so grateful that though I mess up, He will ALWAYS be there. My sadness becomes Joy, my weakness becomes strength. On my knees, I know that I am loved and I will share LOVE.

Each day comes with a new start. Each year comes the same way. As the New Year approaches, my heart is full, and my desire is that EVERYONE knows the love of our Father in Heaven! There is NOTHING we can do or go through that is out of HIS reach and care. Happy New Year Friends!

Striving to sit in His lap more often.

Blessings

A New Heart

1/1/2011

I was looking at my fingernails the other day and was amazed. You see, while going through my treatments last year, my fingernails became very bruised and sore. Finally, after a while, they turned green and eventually I lost 6 of them. This side effect of treatment was very interesting to me.

Fingernails, well, actually toenails too, are made up of fast dividing cells, and all fast dividing cells are affected by chemotherapy. It took quite some time for them to fall off, and even more time for them to come back.

However they did come back! So, while I was observing them, I noticed how healthy they now are! God has completely renewed my nails. What was once decaying, green, dead, He made completely new! He restored them!

This is the beginning of a New Year. What an opportunity we have to allow Our Father in heaven to completely renew us. It starts when we yield all control over to Him. He made us, He designed us, and He knows more than anyone how to restore us!

Therefore, if anyone is in Christ, he is a new creation; old things have passed away; behold, all things have become new. 2 Corinthians 5:17 NKJV

I am praying for a new heart! I am praying that I will yield every part of myself to Him, most of all my heart! My hope is as my heart is yielded, the rest of me will follow. I will allow Him to make the changes in me that will get rid of the old, decaying, dead parts of my life. That He will breathe into me, so that every part of me will be new. When I do this, all of my "new days, new weeks, new months, new years," will be overflowing. I will see how He changes the old, and gives me all that I need to do His will.

His desire is to do this for each of us. He has promised All things will be new. I will trust Him for this. I can't wait to see the results. Just as I saw Him renew my fingernails, and many things in my life this past year. The hardest part is yielding. So I will pray for new eyes, new ears, and a new heart, and the desire to yield it all to Him!

Blessings

Yielding to God
1/7/2011

I was reading the story of Abraham, Sarah, and Hagar in Genesis 16 today. It is the story of Sarah giving Hagar to Abraham so she could bare him a son. Now Hagar was just doing what she was told, she was their servant (Sarah's, actually). She had no choice really. So she does what she is told, and then Sarah starts to treat her poorly because she does what Sarah asks! Has this ever happened to you? I know it has to me. We do the things we are supposed to do, then someone gets upset about it. We can't win. I am sure this is what Hagar must have felt. Later in the story, God speaks to Hagar and comforts her. He knows the situation, what took place. He makes a request of Hagar, and assures her that everything will be okay. Then she says: *"I have seen the One Who sees me!"* WOW!

It is funny to me that we think for one minute that God doesn't see some of things we do, or think, or say, or our circumstances. Of course He does! He is God! Yet we somehow can convince ourselves, (with a little push from the enemy), that He doesn't understand, or really see what is happening to us. Over and over in scripture He constantly reminds us of His love for us. He KNOWS us, and yet still loves us! He is our Creator, how could He not know everything about His creation? He is all knowing.In Matthew 6 it talks about our Father, who knows all secrets. I read in the Psalms:

...For You look deep within the mind and heart, O Righteous God. Psalm 7:9b

While this thought could be a little unnerving, I think it is more comforting. You see, even when we are punished unjustly, or spoken poorly of, He KNOWS! So all the times we feel slighted, or unjustly accused or mistreated, we don't have to wonder if God really saw what took place. If we are not trying to walk in His ways, and doing things that we know He wouldn't want us to, then yeah, unnerving is a good word. He knows the deepest part of us, we are His creation. There are no secrets between God and us. He knew we would mess up, but He also gives us All that we need to try and follow His direction. He looks on our heart. He wants to see a child that is willing to admit when they are wrong, and love and trust Him completely. Sometimes this can appear hopeless. We just don't feel like we measure up. Yet all He asks us to do is to give our hearts completely to Him, and He will do the rest. There is rest and peace when we do this, and more importantly hope. Hope that "The One Who sees" us understands everything.

This little battle of yielding can be won just by realizing Who God is, and there is NOTHING we can hide from Him. Why would we want to anyway? Resting in the fact that He sees me and in spite of me, loves me, and will NEVER give up on me... Now that is HOPE!

Blessings

Words
1/14/2011

I had a conversation recently with a friend about the power that words hold. This past year, dealing with cancer, and having many people encourage me, bless me, pray for me, reminded me of the power of words. Here are some that have been important for me this past year.

When we were given the news of cancer, we immediately asked all the prayer warriors we know to start praying. One sister, praying over me in church, said; "This is not a surprise to God. He knows what you are going through, what you will have to endure, and He is with you!" I held onto these words throughout my treatment. Knowing someone spoke these comforting words over me, got me through some extremely rough days. Thinking of all the people that were lifting me up before the Lord continually filled me with hope and the Bible tells us that "Hope will not disappoint![5]"

There were so many other words such as; trust, faith, love, healing, assurance, peace. My family and friends prayed these words and spoke them over me continually. I am not sure what I would have done had this not been true. There were many songs that had words full of power that I held onto as well. I have shared some of them already in other entries.

Most importantly were the scriptures that I was given both by people and reminded of from the Lord. God's Word is powerful! It is life. He has given it to us for direction, strength, healing, peace. It is true. He cannot lie, and everything He says in is Word is true! Isn't that amazing? Below are some of the scriptures that helped me through. So many were given to me that it would be impossible to list them all. My hope and prayer is that you will take the time to look up these scriptures. That you would be assured of His love for you, and also that He will always be with you. That you will be blessed by His Word. Let your heart, soul, mind, and body be filled with His Word! It is the best thing to hold onto in any kind of struggle, both physically and spiritually.

Isaiah 58: 8, Luke 8:48, Psalm 30:2, Isaiah 53:5, Psalm 103: 1 - 4, Psalm 107: 20, Proverbs 4:22, Exodus 23:25, Mark 11:24, Malachi 4:2, Hebrews 11:6

5   Romans 5:5 NKJV

Like I said, there were so many others too numerous to share in this space.

Words are powerful. Let's strive to be careful of the words we speak to others. Let our words speak life, grace, hope, love, healing into the lives of others! I hope I have done this for y'all!

Blessings

Listening Through The Noise
1/18/2011

Righteousness and justice are the foundation of your throne. Unfailing love and truth walk before you as attendants. Happy are those who hear the joyful call to worship, for they will walk in the light of your presence, Lord. They rejoice all day long in your wonderful reputation. They exult in your righteousness. Psalm 89:14-16 NLT

My prayer is that I will walk in the light of His presence all day long and rejoice in Him. It is very difficult these days to keep our focus on Jesus. We see everything going on around us, and either it helps us to look to Him, or we try and fix things ourselves. Sometimes I am part of the latter group...We will not be able to fix the wrongs in this world with legislation or policies alone, we need Jesus! This world, our nation, our homes need Jesus! Let's listen intently for His voice, and walk with Him. As we do this, we show others the way, and it moves through people, and effects the people around us, and the people they come in contact with, and so on, and so on...

May we all hear His voice today, and lead people in the right direction!

Blessings

Treasure
1/21/2011

MY SON, if you will receive my words and treasure up my commandments within you, making your ear attentive to skillful and godly Wisdom and inclining and directing your heart and mind to understanding [applying all your powers to the quest for it]; Yes, if you cry out for insight and raise your voice for understanding, If you seek [Wisdom] as for silver and search for skillful and godly Wisdom as for hidden treasures, then you will understand the reverent and worshipful fear of the Lord and find the knowledge of [our omniscient] God. Proverbs 2:1-5 AMP

This is packed full of insight. When I was younger, I would hide things from my brothers, that were special to me, because I didn't want them to get it and spoil it or take it from me. Sometimes I would forget about it, and months later, find something that I had hidden. Oh, what joy, what excitement! Do you remember those childhood feelings? The excitement could almost be overwhelming. How much more should my joy be for finding wisdom in The Word of God! Look at what we must do: treasure up His commandments within ourselves, making our ear attentive, applying all our powers to the quest of understanding godly Wisdom.

Cry out for insight! Seek wisdom just as we would for treasure! My goal is to do all of the above, much more than I do now. I am just beginning to understand that Godly Wisdom truly helps me to understand the reverent and worshipful fear of the Lord. I need more of Him every day! I truly want to hide His Word in my heart, and grow closer to Him, and be a really good listener when He is trying to tell me something! Then, of course, act on things when He desire's action from me.

This is a lot to think about, I better get started!

Blessings

Family Life
1/24/2011

A house is built by wisdom and becomes strong through good sense. Through knowledge its rooms are filled with all sorts of precious riches and valuables. Proverbs 24:3-4 NLT

Sometimes the pressure of life is overwhelming. We get so busy with "life" that we forget to notice how "life" is in our homes...That life is so much more important than any other part of life! We are in a battle these days to protect our family time. There are too many things that try and snatch it away from us...work, activities outside the home, etc. We have all felt it before I think. That place that feels like we get up in the morning and get the kids dressed and fed, get them to school, go to work, pick up the kids, feed them dinner, do homework, go to a practice of some sort, get home in time for bath time, and then bed. The next day we get up and start the routine all over again. Not that any of these things are bad in and of themselves. We can get so busy that we don't have time to really experience, love on, share wisdom, funny stories, hugs, kisses, with our family. We don't have time to impart the wisdom and love of Jesus with our children, so they can experience His love, His wisdom, and know Him on their own. We must work hard to make that time happen every day! That time is too important to let "life" snatch it away from us! Of course, if we are where we are supposed to be in our walk with the Lord, it shines out of our everyday life, and spills on our kids, and family.

So, that is good, but we also need to make time to share with them what the Lord is doing, and capable of doing in our lives—it is just so important! Those things are "the precious riches and valuables"! Make special time with your family today, treat them to a listening session! You know what I mean... special "you" time, and special "Jesus" time, and then see what the Lord can do!

When you have experienced something like I did this past year, you realize even more how important it is for that special time with your family. Let's not let another second go by, it's too important. We so need to share Jesus with our families. When we have shared Jesus with them, and know He is the One they will go to first, then we have done the best thing for them. Then they share with their families, and it goes on.

   Blessings

What I have learned...

well at least a few of the things.

2/1/2011

I have learned so much over this past year. It was a tough one, but with the help of God, my family and I made it through. So what have I learned?

Well...

- I learned that I am tougher than I ever could have imagined.

- I really do trust in the Lord, and lean on Him for more than I thought.

- I have learned more information about cancer than I ever wanted to, mostly from personal experience, but also from doing my own research into the disease that tried to wreak havoc on my body.

- I have learned how amazing this body that God created really is.

- I have learned that family is the most wonderful thing, and though I have always known this, it was so evident as we struggled through this together.

- I have learned that when we hide our heart, soul, and mind with the Lord, the enemy can't get in there and confuse us or our circumstances.

- God is my Healer.

- I have amazing friends, whom I was blessed to have praying for me, and sharing with me, crying with me, laughing with me. I am very thankful for all y'all!

- Time is precious. We spend too much time on things that aren't important. Relationships are the most important, and it starts with our relationship with Jesus!

- God's promises are true! If you have ever doubted, ask me, I would love to share with you sometime.

- God's love is bigger than I can comprehend. I am always learning how He loves me more than I can imagine. I want to learn to love that way...

I could probably go on for hours... Though the year was tough, I have learned so many things that I am thankful for. With every difficult circumstance, there is good also. Sometimes it is very hard to see or understand. If we trust that God has our best in mind, this is much easier to do.

Maybe if we try not to approach difficulty kicking and screaming, and trust God to bring us through, we might have the opportunity to help someone else. That is my desire. I hope I have helped someone...

Blessings

God's Word

2/7/2011

For as the rain and snow come down from the heavens, and return not there again, but water the earth and make it bring forth and sprout, that it may give seed to the sower and bread to the eater, So shall My word be that goes forth out of My mouth: it shall not return to Me void [without producing any effect, useless], but it shall accomplish that which I please and purpose, and it shall prosper in the thing for which I sent it. Isaiah 55:10-11 AMP

God's Word is amazing! In the first verse it is compared to rain or snow. It is refreshing, just what the sower needs for his seed to grow. It accomplishes it's purpose! We probably all remember the second verse, it is well known. See how the Amplified Bible puts it? "It will not return without producing any effect!"

Amen! When God speaks, something happens. It is never, ever, useless! It accomplishes God's purpose. I know that I need more of His Word in my heart, and mind.It is life, powerful, important, full of His wisdom and grace. Even though the world might suggest it has no affect or current value, that simply is not true. We need the Bible now, more than ever! We need to help people understand its value, and its effect on our lives. Please pray with me for a deep desire for more of God's Word. We simply need God's purpose in our land, not our own!

I know that we all probably try every year to read the Bible through in a year, or maybe just read something from the Bible every day. Then sometime in March, we slack off, and maybe get discouraged that we didn't keep up with it. Make this year different! The Bible is life to our souls, we need it so much! Let's make it a priority!

I have been reminded over and over, especially this past year, to "hide His Word in my heart!" I want to have His life and strength in me. It is powerful and true. I am so thankful that He is Faithful and His Word is true, because that is what got me through this past season...

Blessings

Being Prepared
2/8/2011

Part of my devotion today was about the bridesmaids being prepared for the coming of the bridegroom. In the story, some of the bridesmaids didn't have enough oil to wait for the bridegroom. They had to leave their post of waiting to go find some place that would sell them more oil... because they weren't prepared, they missed the arrival of the bridegroom, and were not allowed to join the celebration.

There have been many times when I wished I had been more prepared. For instance, not having the camera for a really great photo opportunity. Or not having quite enough money for something because I didn't plan ahead for wanting to purchase something. Or not being able to really enjoy a sunset because of the coolness of the air, and not having enough warm clothing with me. How about missing time with friends and family because of scheduling issues. We have all been there.

Just not as prepared as we would like to have been.

I definitely wasn't prepared for the diagnosis of cancer. No one ever is. We try to do our best to keep ourselves healthy, and then something like this happens. We can't really be completely prepared in the physical for any illness or tragedy. However, we certainly can be prepared in the spiritual realm. How? By spending that much needed time with the Lord. By making sure our relationship with Him is priority and cultivating it every day. Hiding His Word in our hearts, so when we are overwhelmed, we can have the Treasure of His Word to hold onto, and glean from. Jesus used this story to remind us that we don't know the day or hour of His coming again.

So, what we need to do is keep our hearts and minds stayed on Him, and in His Word. Expecting that today could possibly be that day... Having a good relationship with Him and hiding His Word in our hearts helps us through the day to day life as well. Even when illness or tragedy come knocking at the door. We are better prepared to handle illness and tragedy when we are holding onto Him. He has promised to never leave us, to be our Strength, our Healer, our Guide. I am so thankful that I was holding onto Him through my treatments. That I felt Him holding me, and loving me, and being my Strength, when I didn't have any. I wasn't prepared for this illness in the physical, but I had a strong relationship with my Lord, and He was faithful to bring me through.

Do you know Him? Do you depend on Him? If not, I would love to hear from you and share with you about His amazing love for you!

Blessings

Set Apart

2/9/2011

In the Old Testament, in the book of Exodus, it gives us information about how the priests were to be cleansed, anointed, set apart, for their service to the Lord. It even says their clothing was supposed to be beautiful, distinguished, so the people would be able to tell they were different.

Please take a few minutes and read Exodus 28. In verse 36, it says there was a medallion made for Aaron to be worn on his head, that said;
"Set Apart As Holy Unto The Lord."

We know what is said, and happened in the Old Testament, was leading us to Jesus. Jesus became our High Priest, He was "set apart" by God, no one could do what Jesus did. He also says we are "Set Apart As Unto

The Lord", that is what being Holy means.

Some of you were once like that. But you were cleansed; you were made holy; you were made right with God by calling on the name of the Lord Jesus Christ and by the Spirit of our God. 1 Corinthians 6:11

We were made Holy. So what does that mean for us? Should we be wearing robes like the priests of the Old Testament did? Well I don't really think so, but we should definitely look different than everyone else. It is more about our countenance, and what people see our values are, and if they see Jesus in us. How should we be setting ourselves apart? Taking that much needed time with the Lord, clothing ourselves in Him. There is so much that desires our time in this world. The truth of the matter is, we put a lot of stuff we shouldn't into our heads and hearts, that keeps us from being set apart, Holy. If we want to be Holy, to look more like Jesus, we need to make the effort to do the things we know we can do, what we are responsible for, and then rest in the Lord for perfecting it in us. Asking for His help every day, spending time with Him, listening to Him, reading His Word.

These are the things we can do to set ourselves apart from this world and draw us closer to Him. If we spend time doing these things, we have much less time to get in trouble with the things the world offers, that seem to pull us away from Him, and keep us from reaching the goal of being "set apart!"

I know I want to be "Set Apart As Unto The Lord!" I want everyone to know I belong to Him. I want everyone to know His love for them, and the blessings of a life given completely to Him. Our lives here on this earth will be full, complete, and safe with Him, even during the rough seasons.

Living holy is becoming my goal every day, I hope it is yours as well.

Blessings

Why I Share
2/10/2011

I spent most of 2010 fighting cancer. Actually, I know the Lord fought the battle for me. I had a team of amazing doctors, and my family and friends were praying for me every day! I am blessed to be able to say today that I am cancer free. So why do I keep doing blogs?

Well, my heart is to help people. I love people. I love to people watch, to be at the mall during the Christmas season, to be in a park, and watch people interact. It is my heart to help people in any way I can. So I write. I love to put my thoughts down on paper (or in the computer).I am hoping when I share here, that it touches someone, and maybe they will see they are not alone. I share a lot about my walk with the Lord, because He is my life. I would not know what to do, or what I would have done, without the Lord to help me get through last year. I may not be the smartest or wisest, but I share from my life and heart, and sometimes it just helps to know someone else is experiencing the same thing. I hope when I share my feelings that someone who has felt the same way will see, and know someone understands. I also hope when I share how the Lord has helped me work through my feelings, or how He showed up and carried me through the rough spots, that others will know He will do the same for them as well. He is so important to me that I want to share this Friend with others.

So there you have it...My desire is to be a blessing and maybe a help to others.

Blessings

My Grandma
2/12/2011

My earliest memories of my grandma include my grandpa, but he passed when I was very young. So while I cherish those memories, I have a childhood full of memories of grandma. I remember spending the night with her, and staying up until 11 pm. (which was very late for me). We would watch the late movie, and if we happened to fall asleep, that was okay. Sometimes she would make popcorn, mostly she would have ice cream, and some sort of cookie or cake!

I remember when I was a little older, making chocolates with her during the holidays. This candy was so wonderful. It was truffle - like, and a walnut sat on top of each one. She also made chocolate covered cherries with an amazing filling. She was also very well known for her coleslaw! It was really amazing, and I watched her make it on many occasions. I loved her coleslaw so much, it is hard for me to eat any other! I am sad to say the candy and coleslaw recipes are forever gone. For some reason none of the family ever had her write them down.

From my earliest memories we went to church together. My mom and dad didn't go to church with me when I was young. I knew I could always go with grandma, and sometimes I would go out to eat lunch with her and one of her friends. In one of her last homes, I remember my whole family going over there and having Sunday dinner that consisted of roast and mashed potatoes, gravy, green beans, and some kind of rolls. She had an old television, and my dad would sit in her comfortable chair and watch a game of some sort, while she made last minute dinner preparations. My mom and I would help, but grandma usually had it all under control.

One of my favorite memories is sitting by grandma on the bench while she played hymns on her organ. I would sing at the top of my lungs while she played. She would tell me I had a beautiful voice, and said I should sing nice and loud! I believe I learned to love singing from the time I spent next to grandma. I asked her one time why she didn't play in church, she said she played just because she enjoyed it, and wasn't good enough to play in front of anyone. I don't believe that is true. She played really well...However, I don't remember her ever playing in front of anyone but me. I could see Jesus in her eyes, and just feel His presence when she played. That's why she did it. It was one way she worshiped the Lord. She actually worshiped Him in almost everything she did.

She knew Him well, and it showed in everything she did!

She was also very stubborn. As she grew older, she insisted on doing things for herself, and I remember her having a hard time giving up driving. She was a very independent, strong woman. If asked, my parents would have said I took after my grandma.

I remember watching her hands when she cooked, played, washed dishes. I loved her hands! We would hold hands when we took walks, and they were comforting to me. When I was younger, and didn't know better, I thought if I just watched closely enough, I could learn to play like she did. Well I never did. However, I noticed the other day my hands do look a little like grandmas! I am so excited! I am sure there are other parts of me as well, especially my walk with the Lord, that look like grandma.

My prayer is I will pass some wonderful memories to my girls, and their children! I hope when my grandchildren look back, they will have amazing memories of our time together. I hope I shine Jesus to them in everything I do, and they will attribute some of who they are to me... and they too, will shine Jesus to generations to come!

Thank you, grandma, for sharing Jesus with me, and being such a special part of who I am today!

Blessings

The Thief

2/14/2011

There were two thieves crucified along with Jesus. They'd been tried and convicted. One went out cursing and swearing oaths, the other realized the error of his ways and cried out to Jesus, "Remember me when you come into your Kingdom." And Jesus, seeing past his circumstance and into his newly changed heart, replied, "Surely today you will be with me in paradise.[6]"

AMAZING! Before he left this world, he repented from his heart, and Jesus knew it. Grace was given to this man in his last moments as he acknowledged Christ the Lord. We don't know how he lived his life, what his "works" were, just that he repented. I believe this happens more than we know. If we believe on the Lord Jesus, we will be saved! AMEN!

6   Luke 23:42-43 NKJV

Waiting until we are in our last moments to acknowledge Jesus is not necessarily God's perfect plan. Abundant, eternal life is available to us for our whole lives, not just for our heavenly eternity. Though if a person finds their self at the end of the line and finally God's truth sinks in and they turn to Him, even with their last breath of confession, He will hear them and meet them right there. We don't know what the next minute holds and death sometimes comes when least expected, then, our eternal reward.

God's love is so amazing He wants us to experience it here and now, in this life as well as in eternity. He makes all things new, and clean, and full. He came so we might have life more abundantly! If we choose Him now, before we are breathing our last, oh how amazing life is! We are not perfect, so life isn't perfect, but with Jesus, we have all the help we need to run this race! Won't you consider opening your heart to Him today? Asking for forgiveness, and help in navigating this journey we are all on? He is waiting for you right now!

Blessings

Focus

2/20/2011

One of my favorite stories is in Mark 5, it is about a man Jesus set His focus on. Jesus and His disciples had been very busy during the day, and evening had come, Jesus was tired, but there was still someone who needed Him, so He directed the disciples to cross over by boat to the other side of the sea. After a great storm in which the disciples feared for their lives, (Chapter 4), they arrived at the other side. Immediately after reaching shore, they were approached by a man who was possessed by a legion of demons, and this poor man was miserable. He lived among the tombs, and all the time he hit himself and screamed because of the demons. Oh how this hurt the heart of Jesus. So while the disciples didn't understand why Jesus might have demanded they go to the other side of sea in the first place, Jesus had set His focus on helping this man, and no distraction of any kind, (wind, storm, personal weariness) would make a difference in reaching him.

I am so thankful for the focus of the Lord. He delivered and healed this man and got back in the boat to go back to where they came from. Jesus had set His focus for a journey that didn't make much sense to anyone else for the sake of one poor, lost man.

God does this all the time. He is God, and He not only keeps the world spinning, which I am sure takes an amazing amount of focus, He also focuses on you and me. Not one detail of our life, circumstances, hurts, diseases, does He miss. He is so focused on you and me, that He reminds us over and over that He loves us and knows all about us. His focus is set on a relationship with each of us, personally. That is the desire of His heart!

Oh how I am thankful this past year Jesus had His focus set on me, and my need for healing. I know I am not the only one He was focusing on, which is so amazing! Many people cry out to the Lord, and He hears them, and meets them right where they are, like He did me. God is Good, isn't He? If we can focus our hearts and minds on Jesus, and our relationship with Him, we are in the best place. Not only will we be able to see more of His love for us, but it also sets us up to do what we were put here on this earth to do, walk in our destiny, like the man Jesus healed who ended up taking the gospel to that entire region.

I am learning to set my focus on the Lord first, and it teaches me to be able to focus on others, and the things that Jesus wants me to do in this lifetime, and to be all He wants me to be!

Blessings

The Past

2/23/2011

I was thinking about my past. How I remember my childhood, and the people who have made a difference in my life. There are so many, I am so thankful for. I hope I can learn from the past, and not repeat the same mistakes again. However, I do not want to live in the past. Sometimes we spend so much time thinking how it used to be, we miss what God is doing today and we also miss the hope of a better tomorrow. I don't really get people who really can't seem to move out of the past. They want to keep something that just isn't relevant anymore. I know there are really good things from my past, like the day I met my hubby, and the day my girls were born. It is best to cherish these memories and live for today and the future.

My recent past was bumpy at times. I would definitely wake up and wish the day would go by quickly, so it would be over, and I could go back to bed. I also learned how precious each moment is, and to make the most of it.

I want to keep moving forward! I know that I would not trade what I have learned in the past year for anything. However, I could choose to let the illness I endured define who I am. I talked about this with a friend the other day. She also has endured cancer, and we were saying how you get so used to taking pills, getting poked, visiting doctors, watching your blood count, taking your temperature, that when it is over, you aren't sure what to do next. In a way, it becomes so much a part of your life while you are going through it, when you are done, you wonder now what?

I know, and so does she, that we have come through something big, and we both want to make every moment count, and help everyone we can. First of all, I hope I can lead people to the Source, Jesus. Y'all know I believe He is the Reason I am healed today. Second, I am going to find every way possible to spend wonderful moments with my family and give myself to them in every way I can. Third, I am taking every chance I get to talk with people, and love on people who are enduring an illness or tragedy. I pray every day for a chance to share, I know the Lord will open the doors I am supposed to step through. I am also going to come along side others who are working so hard to find a cure for cancer. I hope to be able to participate in one of the many walks to find a cure this year.

So while the past is good, I am looking forward, and moving forward, to keep myself on the path God is revealing to me every day and praying I can love people, and look at them the way He does.

Blessings

Becoming A Next Gen Cheerleader!
3/3/2011

Ed and I have been spending time with some wonderful young people who are trying to listen to the Lord and be who God wants them to be. We are literally the oldest people in the room when we meet, what an odd new feeling for us. While I was listening to one young woman talk, I realized that I had thought the same things through the years. I just wanted to hug her and tell her she is okay, and she is on the right path! Then I realized, maybe that is why God has put us all together. If all we do is encourage, and help them see the potential they have, and that it is definitely okay to dream BIG for the Lord, give them wings to accomplish ALL they are supposed to, and not squelch what the Spirit is doing in their midst, we have done something good.

On our way home from the meeting, I was sadden by the fact that our generation has dropped the ball in relationship with those coming up behind us. We didn't want to let go of some power that we thought we possessed, which actually wasn't ours in the first place. We held so tightly to our tradition, and our way of thinking, that we failed to allow good change to happen. We spoke words of discouragement instead of life, and we effectively told these kids that they were too young, too inexperienced to know what God is doing. In some cases we have been so discouraging and so unlike Jesus that we have driven them away from the body of Christ, because all they can see are a bunch of dysfunctional organizations controlled by people who could care less if they come or go.

Our desire is to be encouragers, releasers, and cheer leaders for the next generation. Help people (young and old) to understand that the "God Ideas" as Ed likes to call them, are exciting, and help them realize they really can accomplish their dreams, then, help them 'take off!'

As we get older, we are supposed to be a little more experienced, wiser, however that does not mean we know everything. We should NEVER squeeze the life, love, excitement of a dream, out of someone younger than ourselves. I hope I can always encourage and be a mentor and pass down Godly wisdom to people who haven't been around the block quite as many times as I have. My prayer is to leave behind a good legacy, to be a person who allowed kids to dream and hope and run and fly!

The lesson I'm learning is to be who I am, to listen, to pray, to encourage, and be who God called me to be... even if I am twice as old as everyone else in the room.

Blessings!

The Right Path

3/15/2011

I was reading today in Numbers about the children of Israel. They were getting a group together to go back to the land where they had been slaves prior to God's miraculous deliverance. Never mind all God had done for them, they whined and complained and decided that they had it better back in Egypt.

God spoke to Moses and told him to tell the children of Israel because of their complaining, and I think forgetfulness, they would not be entering the promised land. When they realized what they were doing was going to get the promised land taken away from them, they decided to change their tune. In the scripture it says they decided, "Oh alright, we will go into the land God is giving us", like it was such a chore... Actually, they knew they were going to lose something, so they decided to change their ways. Only this time it was too late. Now God wasn't going to go before them, He told them they were going to be punished by wandering in the wilderness for 40 years. God is so long suffering, merciful, that He wasn't just going to wipe this people out, He was going to give them still another chance, but they would have to wander in the wilderness first. He said nothing about leaving them... He knew what was best, and was trying to help these guys out, just as He had done numerous times before.

We are so much like the children of Israel. We want our way so much, even if we don't see God in it, we think we know best, and we are going to pursue on our own. If I have learned anything over the years, especially in this last year, it is that I don't want to be where God isn't! I don't want to go down a road without holding His hand. Sometimes we really need to look at the direction we are going, the one we are choosing, and decide if we really see the Lord on our path. If not, we need to GET OFF THAT ROAD. Change our course, do something different. The children of Israel did this many times, and you know what? God didn't give up on them. If we are truly trying to pursue God, and His ways, He will direct us, and then our choice is to follow, or not. We won't always make the right choice, but God is a God of second chances, or third chances, or fourth chances... He loves us so much, that though we disappoint Him, He won't leave us!

I am so thankful for His love and direction in my life! I want to please Him in all I do, but when I fail, I know that I can come to Him with my brokenness and He is there to love me, hold me, fix me. Amen!

Blessings

Balaam

3/15/2011

Sometimes I feel like the donkey in the story of Balaam[7]. Poor thing... he was just trying to keep Balaam from making a serious mistake, and Balaam couldn't see it. Have you experienced times when you are trying to do the right thing, and protect someone you love, and it feels like they just keep beating you up for it? I know I have, and it hurts! Sometimes people are very stubborn... I know I am. There are many times I feel like Balaam as well. But, I think for the most part, this is a good thing. In Balaam's case, God was really trying to get his attention, and keep him from doing something that he shouldn't have been doing. Now, while I think I do this quite often, I am certainly glad that God keeps trying so hard to get my attention! God really

---

7   Numbers 22:1-39

did go to extremes here to help Balaam out. If you read the story it is quite comical. God even had the donkey speak to Balaam!

AND Balaam still wasn't getting it! I wonder if an animal spoke to me like that, if I would be in awe, or beat it like Balaam? How many times do we not listen to the still small voice of the Lord, and He has to go to extremes to get our attention?

I guess I was just continuing my thought from the previous blog. The Good News is God won't let go of us! I pray that my stubbornness doesn't always get in the way of what God is trying to teach me. I want to walk with Him, because over and over He has proven Himself to me, and more importantly, HE loves me. He will always have what is best for me in mind. You know it must have been hard for Balaam to keep trying to squeeze by in the direction he wasn't supposed to be going. I don't want to do that! I want to walk with Him, let Him lead. After all, that is the best dance move right?

Going to try and put my listening ears on every morning, and be a better dance partner!

Blessings

Looking for Protection?

3/19/2011

When you think that you finally have something under control, or you have conquered it, the enemy really tries to get in there and mess with your head and your heart. I am sure we have all been there many more times than we care to admit. It hurts the heart of God, and the truth of the matter is it hurts us too, when we allow the enemy an "in!" Satan's whole job is to seek to devour and destroy us. If we open the door for him, he is definitely going to enter. He wants to separate us from God. Satan wants to try and convince us we have done something so completely awful that God will not forgive, nor continue to love us. NOT TRUE! He is the father of lies, and that is something we need to continue to tell ourselves!

So how do we protect ourselves against the deceiver?

It starts with completely surrendering everything to the Lord. There is nothing we should hold onto, except Jesus. When we realize the direction we are heading, or the decision we are making, or the thoughts we are thinking, are not what God wants of us, admit it to the Lord. Ask for forgiveness, because He will forgive us. Decide we want to look more like our Father in Heaven. Desire to be so close to Him, and love Him, so everything we want to do, or think is pleasing to Him. Of course, there are choices we make as well. Decide it is more important for us to be close to Jesus than to watch that movie, or lie, or spend time with someone we know we shouldn't. Everything we do in secret, God sees. I am not sure where we ever got the idea we can keep secrets from the Lord. He sees everything. He knows our thoughts even before we do. It is Who God is!

So we should realize that what we think we are doing in secret, really isn't. If we truly love the Lord, we would think more carefully about breaking His heart with the things we do. It is so important for us to take time each day with Him. Not only does He desire this so much, but we need it! We need to spend time reading His Word, and listening, and worshiping! I have mentioned before that we want to spend time with people we care about, how much more so it should be with the Lord.

I just had a funny thought, there is a song called "Waiting On A Woman" by Brad Paisley. The whole idea of the song is that if you are a man, you will probably do this a lot. In the song he suggests if you are in love with this woman, it is definitely worth it. Well, God loves us so much more than anyone ever could, and you know what? He is waiting on us all the time! He waits for us to spend time with Him, to call on Him, to desire to be more like Him!

I am so thankful that Jesus made a way for me to approach our Father In Heaven! I am so blessed, and overwhelmingly thankful that He loves me more than I know! I am confident when I make a mistake, He sees, and if I ask, He forgives. I am also confident that Greater is He Who is in me, than he who is in the world (the enemy)! Amen!

Blessings

Uncomplicate Our Relationships, Speak Well.

3/21/2011

I have been a wife for many years, in fact I have been married longer than I was single. During this time, I have learned a few things about people, particularly women. And the first thing, and it pretty much goes without saying, is, relationships can be complicated at times. Unfortunately, much of what complicates our marital relationships are issues of our own creation, like how we talk to and about our spouse.

I have been with women who put their husband or fiancé down. Maybe it's just in fun, but words mean things, and they have power. They can wound both the person you are joking about and yourself if you are careless with them.

Men, the woman you are engaged or married to, needs to know that you only have eyes for them! EVEN if they appear to be sure of themselves and act as if they don't care. The world has somehow twisted our minds to think we can assure someone we love them more than any other, and it is still okay to be flirtatious with others. It's not.

Recently in church, we were talking about love and the marriage relationship. If we love someone, we should honor and respect them, always want what is best for them, and love them unconditionally. How do we show respect for our spouse when we talk in a manner that we shouldn't about the opposite sex? The enemy would like us to believe it is okay, because he doesn't want us to have strong relationships. Satan would say that it is the way of the world, that everybody does it, and that it is harmless fun. But does it make sense that we want the best for our spouse, then say things that suggest we really don't respect them all that much? We wonder why the divorce rate is so high...

We all have the ability to make choices about what we say and how we treat the people closest to us. My prayer is that I will honor my husband, show him ALWAYS there is no one I love or want more than him! He does this for me all the time! If we can do our best to honor, love, respect our spouse, and others close to us, I think our relationships would be a bit less complicated.

Blessings

Finally

3/19/2012

I feel as if I have been through quite a bit in the last 2 years. Being diagnosed with cancer just tipping the iceberg. From the very beginning of my diagnosis, I knew Jesus had given me a Word that I would be healed. Of course I kept praying it would be instantly, and then I prayed it would be without surgery. However, I also decided in my heart that however He chose to heal me, was okay with me! I trusted Him with my life, and though I had all the conventional treatments, He did heal me!!! It's been a about eighteen months since I received my first *"no evidence of disease"*, on the various scans and tests the doctors have ordered! All clear for going on two years!!

I praise Jesus for healing my body, and drawing me closer to Him! I love Him, and will share what He has done in me with anyone who will listen!

Tomorrow is another mile stone in this healing process. It's a big step and a little scary, but I'm ready I think! I have a peace that can only come from the Lord, and I know the timing is really good to go through with this. I am continually thankful for everyone who says they are praying for me, and I ask that you continue to do so.

The Lord has been reminding me about peace the past few days. He is our Peace. He can bring comfort and love like no other. He holds us when we are unsure, and reminds us He is Faithful! He has promised to always be with us, and never, ever leave us! I'm holding onto these promises for tomorrow, and the days of recovery following.

No matter what circumstance you find yourself in, no matter all the chaos of the world, Jesus loves you, and He hears when you call on Him. He will never leave or forsake you! His love is unconditional and never ending! Hold onto Him!

Blessings

New Every Morning

11/24/2019

**The steadfast love of the Lord never ceases; his
mercies never come to an end;
they are new every morning; great is your
faithfulness. Lamentations 3:22-23 ESV**

This passage might be the best way to describe my on-going journey. Every word is true. Life is precious, and life with Jesus is the most precious, because it never ends. During this journey two of my fellow warriors, Christina Milan and Kim Holmes, women who gave me strength and for whom I prayed without ceasing, finished their earthly journey and went to be with Jesus. Their battle was won by their mortality being swallowed up by life, as it says in 2 Corinthians:

For we who are in this tent groan, being burdened,

not because we want to be unclothed, but further clothed, that mortality may be swallowed up by life. 2 Corinthians 5:4 NKJV

Christina and Kim, warriors and heroes to many hundreds of people like me, fought the good fight and kept the faith and beat that evil disease once and for all. I pray for their loved ones because we're never ready to let someone go, at least not when they are so young and strong.

Me, I don't know why God healed me in this life rather than the next. I might think to ask Him, but I probably won't. I will just honor His mercy by living simply and gratefully. I will try and honor ladies like Christina and Kim, my own mother and mother-in-law, women whose lives were cut short by disease, by serving others and keeping their memories alive by telling of their stories. Stories of the goodness of God and the love of Jesus.

Since 2010, I have not only got to see my grandsons mature into fine young men, but I have also gained two son-in-laws, and five granddaughters, with another on the way! I've enjoyed beautiful intimacy with my husband of forty years. And I have learned that the sufferings of this life are not worthy to be compared to the glory of knowing Jesus, my Lord and Savior, my Healer and Friend.[8]

---

8   Romans 8:18

Gallery

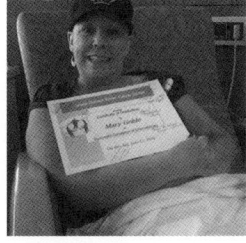

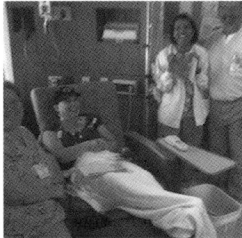

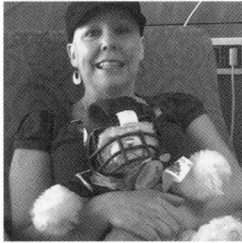

MaryAnn Goble